Low

Soul and Supersoul

(A thorough study of God and his creations, based on Hindu Scriptures)

Jasnita Walia

DK's Books For All

(an imprint of Low Price Publications)
Delhi-110052

Published by
DK's Books For All
A-6, Nimri Commercial Centre,
Near Ashok Vihar Phase-IV,
Delhi-110052
Phones: 011-27302453, Fax: 011-47061936
e-mail: info@Lppindia.com
website: www.Lppindia.com

First Published 2010
ISBN 10 : 81-7386-284-2
ISBN 13: 978-81-7386-284-7

Printed at
D. K. Fine Art Press Pvt. Ltd.
Delhi-110052

Contents

What is God?

Every religion defines God in different ways, but God is one and the same. All-powerful spiritual energy that prevails everywhere. God is formless. He does not have any form, but it has the power to create any form for him and others. He is in the form of blissful and soothing light, just like the light of Sun, but its not hot like Sun. Its light is calm, cool, and peaceful. Its not blazing hot like fire. God has abundant powers.

His powers are defined in the word "God" himself. The word "G" stands for "Generator", "O" stands for "Operator" and "D" stands for "Destroyer", therefore God is the generator, operator and destroyer of the entire universe. God is so powerful that he can create human and animal bodies and then destroy them within a moment, he can create millions of suns, moons, planets and stars and destroy them as per his will.

God creates bodies, sends souls in them, thereafter perishes the bodies and gives rewards and punishments to the souls according to their previous deeds. To understand God and his creations better, lets take the example of the Sun and the Stars. God is like Sun and souls are like stars. God is the supreme soul, the leader of all souls of the entire universes that God has created with his energy. God keeps on creating and destroying the worlds with his energy. God creates human bodies and sends the star like souls in them, so that the human body could function efficiently. The soul is like the battery of the body. The body gains life when the soul enters into it and becomes dead, when the soul leaves the body. The body can't function without the existence of the soul. The soul is the part of the God's supreme energy.

God expands his energy and divides it into small parts. He creates suns, moons, planets and various universes with his energy. Apart from this, God creates administrators to grant boons and punishments to the human beings according to their deeds. He has created demigods like Goddess Lakshmi to grant boon of wealth to the people, God Ganpati, to grant wisdom and prosperity and other Gods like Yama and Shani to grant punishments to people for their deeds that go against the laws of nature. After having made the human being, God wants him to obey his word and lead his life according to the laws of nature, if you go against the laws of nature; you are punished for the same. Just take the example of a person, who does not eliminate the wastes of the body before 7 A.M., he suffers constipation or heaviness of the stomach; if one does not take a bath for a day, he feels dull and remains low in spirits the whole day and if he doesn't take bath for months together, body lice begin to travel on his body.

The consequence of the wrong deed is always bad. God forbids the deeds that go against his will. He wants us to lead a clean life from heart, mind, body and soul. We should clean our body from wastes and dirt and mind from the pollution of negative emotions like hate, lust, jealousy and pride. As we clean our body with soap and water, the same way, we should clean our mind with prayers to Almighty God and virtuous deeds. Everyone in this world is a Sinner. The dirt of our sins causes us sufferings. When we pray to God or chant his holy names, the dirt of our sins tends to reduce gradually. With the reduction of the negativity of the sins, our sufferings begin to decrease with the passage of time. The dirt of sins does not reduce immediately. It takes time. It all depends upon the quality of your spiritual and righteous deeds. The more you pray to God, the lighter shall you become on the burden of your wrong deeds. The Sinner who is overloaded with the burdens of sins is bound to suffer heavy punishments. People who don't pray to God are Sinners. Not to pray to the creator of the universe goes against the laws of nature. If we don't pray to God, we can't reduce the negativity of our sins, and when we are not able to reduce the negativity of sins, we are bound to suffer punishments in the form of sufferings, in this world and the world beyond after death. Therefore utter this small prayer, with closed eyes to God everyday "O beloved father, kindly grant Wisdom, Success, Prosperity, reasonable Wealth, Happiness and Salvation to us, our children, friends, relatives and the entire mankind."

Soul and Mammon

When the creator expands his energy and divides it into tiny souls, he plans to send them into different bodies, according to their past deeds. In case, the creator is creating the world for the first time and there is no account of any souls' past deeds, then he creates one man and one woman to generate the entire species of human beings with them, as per his own will, after that, the whole accounts of everyone's deeds are kept by the administrators of justice and the soul is granted punishments and rewards according to the accounts of their deeds. The soul may take human form or become an animal according to his deeds.

When the soul takes human form and comes in contact with mammon, he becomes so obsessed with mammon that he forgets his relationship with Almighty God. The soul is otherwise clean and pure, but when it takes human form and descends in this world, it becomes selfish, proud and passionate. The human being lusts for beautiful things, persons, luxuries and materialistic things of life. It becomes crazy for more and more things. It becomes jealous of others and keeps on finding faults in other souls, ignoring all his follies. It becomes haughty with wealth and success. The human being commits the most heinous of crimes for his vested interests. He kills, murders, rapes, slaughters other people, without knowing the consequences he would suffer for doing so. In fact, the Sinner commits sin, because he doesn't fear of getting caught for it. The smuggler thinks that no one would know, if he does things here and there and earn good profits from them, the terrorists thinks, what if I leave a bomb secretly in a particular place, who shall sense, what I am doing, the rapist thinks that everyone shall blame the girl considering her characterless, and I shall be saved from the punishments. The Sinner commits the most heinous of crimes, thinking that he shall be saved from the defamation in the society and punishments, as per the laws of the nature. But God's laws do not allow the Sinner to flee away Scot free. The Sinner is bound to suffer punishments for his sinful deeds, whether in this world or the world beyond.

The Lord of Justice does not spare him. In fact, the Sinner commits sins, due to the darkness of ignorance. The God sends messengers of peace on the Earth, to show the right path to the mankind, and eliminate the darkness of ignorance by lighting up the torch of knowledge. The messengers of God are God-like, as they are similar to God and possess the same qualities of God, like humility, kindness, purity and forgiveness. They are the ocean of knowledge and are all-powerful like God, that is why they are also referred as "GOD" by the people of the world. The messengers of God are more powerful then demigods. They have more powers than them. Therefore, they are called God-like spiritual beings. Their mission is to eliminate the sufferings of the mankind and grant them the knowledge about God, their relationship with God and in what way they can attain happiness in this world and the world beyond. To be brief, a soul has to withdraw itself from the temptations of mammon, and meditate on God, if it wants to dwell in peace with God. One must keep on doing efforts in the right direction and leave the fruits on God. This is the right way of life.

The World is a Mirror

The world reflects back what we give to it. When we are kind and loving towards poor, we are respected in this world, when we become cruel and selfish, we are defamed.

The world is the mirror of our deeds. It reflects in a good and bad way.

In fact, God has made the opposite of everything to maintain equilibrium in the world. If there is a male, there is a female to support him, if there is an evil spirit to give trouble to people, there is demigod to give relief from his sufferings, if there is Proton, according to the Laws of Chemistry, there is Neutron too, if there is sickness there is treatment, if the heavy load of sins cause us sufferings, the chanting of Almighty God's name give us relief from all the sufferings. There is a positive side of every negativity and so on. Some of us don't believe in evil spirits but then we are ignorant of this fact. All the scriptures of the world including Hindu Scriptures have stated this truth, that evil spirit do dwell in the world of their own.

In fact, a person who dies a sudden death in an accident or commits suicide becomes an evil spirit. An evil spirit does not have a body like us. It does not have Earth and Water element in its body. It is made up of Air, Sky and Sun. It can fly at any place within some time. It can walk into the closest doors, as its body is made up of air. The evil spirits are created by God, to grant punishment to the human souls for not worshipping him. The evil spirit can enter into the human body and make the person do things in the way they want them to do. They control their brain, hypnotise them and make them behave in a certain way that may be harmful to their career and life. A true worshipper of God or demigod has the ability to grant the person freedom from evil spirit, as their powers are higher then them. The evil spirit can also get freedom and salvation with prayers, meditation and chanting of holy names of God. The birth of an animal, low caste person, or the punishment imparted to evil spirits is all the result of our past deeds and we can get spared from the punishment only by virtuous deeds, that is a universal truth, that none of us can deny.

World is a mirror, as it reflects back our deeds.

Lord Brahma—The Creator

Initially, the whole world was dark and void. There was nothing in the world, except God. Then Almighty God thought of creating a world full of zest and activities. Thus, he created Brahma, the Spiritual Administrator, who was given the task of creating the entire Universe. There is a legend behind the creation of Lord Brahma. Lord Vishnu, who is also called the operator of the world, was created by Almighty God in a divine form. While Vishnu was asleep in the water, a lotus flower, sprouted from his navel. It was an extraordinarily beautiful lotus that had many petals and its stem shone like a thousand of Suns. Brahma took birth from the cells of the Lotus flower. Brahma was confused as he didn't know who was his creator and what was he supposed to do. Brahma thought that perhaps he might get the answers to his questions if he could find the centre of the Lotus. Brahma descended down the stem of the Lotus and wandered around for a hundred years, but still he could not find the centre of the flower. He wandered around for another hundred years but could not find the centre of the Lotus flower. All of a sudden he heard a voice "Brahma do meditation". Thereafter Brahma meditated for twelve years. After twelve years, Vishnu appeared before Brahma in his divine form. Brahma asked him to tell his identity. Instead of directly replying the question, Vishnu replied that the great Lord Vishnu had created him and he was the same Lord Vishnu, from whose body, he took birth.

Brahma still did not believe in his words and began to fight with him. While they were engaged in fighting, Lord Shiva's image appeared before them in a shining form. Vishnu said that now that a third being has appeared, they must stop fighting and find out who he was. Vishnu further added that Brahma should adopt the form of a Swan and go up, while he shall become a Boar and go down. They wandered a four thousand years but could not find the third being. After that they returned to the same place from where they had started off and began to pray with faith. They prayed for a hundred years. After the completion of hundred years, the sound of OM was heard and a being with five faces and ten arms appeared in front of them. Vishnu said that it was good that Brahma and he had been fighting for such a long time, which was the reason, why Shiva had appeared before them. Lord Shiva replied that they were all the three parts of the same entity. Brahma was appointed as the Creator, Vishnu was Operator and Lord Shiva was the Destroyer of the world. Thereafter Shiva disappeared and Brahma and Vishnu came to their original forms.

Thereafter Brahma began to pray. From the powers of his meditation, he created several sages. Among them, the prominent sages were Kardama, Daksha and Marichi. Sage Marichi's son was Kashyapa and Daksha had sixty daughters out of which thirteen were married to Kashyapa. The children of Kashyapa and there daughters became gods, demons, birds, snakes and so on. This was how the world was created. Even the Vedas, Upanishads and Puranas state that nobody except Almighty God is perfect. All the other gods and demigods, who are the manifestation of the energy of Supreme God, may have abundant powers, but yet they commit follies like human beings. Lord Brahma too committed a folly by developing physical relations with Goddess Saraswati, the Goddess of Wisdom and Learning. Goddess Saraswati was born out of the body of Brahma, and thus she was his daughter, but he committed a mistake by developing physical relations with her. Thereafter, we can't expect perfection from human beings or gods, except from Almighty God, from which every god, demon and living being originates.

The Hindu Scriptures state that there was nothing in the beginning except darkness. The demons originated from the darkness and the gods were created in the day. The darkness represents all the negative traits like hatred, anger, and lust, while light represents, truthfulness and peace. A maxim states "TAMSO MA JYOTIRGAMAYA". That means O Lord lead us from the darkness to light.

Lord Vishnu—The Operator

Jai Jai Dharmidhar Shruti Sagar,

Jayati Padmadhar Sadguna Agar.

Translation: O Sustainer of the Earth, O Ocean of Knowledge, O Lotus wielder. You are the mine of all virtues. Victory to thee Lord. Lord Vishnu is the operator of the entire universe. He is the expansion of the Supreme Light of God. God has created Lord Brahma, Lord Vishnu and Lord Shiva for the creation, operation and destruction of the entire world. Vishnu is like God, pure, blissful and forgiving. His consort is Goddess Lakshmi, the Goddess of Wealth. Vishnu is called Avatar in the Hindu mythology. "Avatar" means descent in Sanskrit i.e. the higher beings like Vishnu descend on Earth, whenever there is a fall in moral and spiritual values. According to the Hindu scriptures there were 10 major avatars of Lord Vishnu. They were: The Fish, Tortoise, Boar, Man-Lion, Dwarf, Parashuram (Ram with the Axe), Lord Ram, Lord Krishna, Buddha and Kalki.

The Fish Incarnation

The world is bound to destroy, when the negative energy of sins gets accumulated in the universe. The sins committed by the human kind are the major cause of all sufferings. Lord Vishnu took the form of a fish to give this lesson to the world. The story of Lord Vishnu's incarnation as a fish is given below.

Once upon a time, there lived a king named Manu, whose father was Vaivaswal (the Sun). One day, Manu found a small fish in his hands, while taking a bath. The fish spoke to him, saying that it was so small and thus was frightened to be in the river. Thereafter, it requested to him to place it in a small container. Manu took it home and placed it in a jar. The fish began to grow rapidly and finding the jar too small to accommodate, it requested Manu to find something larger. Manu kept in a pond, but after some time, it too became small for it, thereafter Manu placed the fish in River Ganga, yet, the river became too small for its size, since it was growing rapidly in larger size. Finally Manu placed the fish in the ocean. The fish told him that the world was shortly to be destroyed by the natural disasters because the time had come for it to be purified, therefore advised him to build up a ship, with a rope attached to it and take on board the seven benevolent sages and all the seeds of life, when the flood comes, and warned them to begin to descend when the waters receded, or they would not be able to leave the peak. While leaving, the fish disclosed the fact that it was Vishnu in the form of a fish and thereafter disappeared. Besides the fish incarnation, Lord Vishnu also took the forms of Tortoise, Boar, Man-Lion, Dwarf, Parashuram, Lord Ram, Lord Krishna and Lord Buddha. The basic purpose for which a higher spiritual entity like Vishnu descends in this world, is to set-up right corners, and to make the intelligence of the human being work in a right way.

In the incarnation of Lord Buddha, Vishnu says on that one should adopt the eight-fold path of life i.e.:

1. Right views
2. Right intention
3. Right speech
4. Right action
5. Right livelihood
6. Right effort
7. Right mindfulness, and
8. Right concentration

It is said that Lord Vishnu is yet to be born in as "Kalki", who shall take birth in a Brahman's family and shall be extremely powerful and intelligent. He shall fight valiantly against the evil elements to set-up righteousness in the world.

Lord Vishnu is worshipped by innumerable people belonging to Hindu religion. Some of the temples dedicated to Lord Vishnu are: —

1. Lakshmi Narayana Temple, Jaipur—The Birlas constructed this magnificent temple in Jaipur. It is built near Moti Doongri. It is an alluring sight to behold, when obsessed in the evening in the midst of bright lights. The lightening effect gives it a different look.

2. Vaman Temple, Khajuraho—The Vaman Temple is situated in Khajuraho. This elegant temple is dedicated to the Dwarf incarnation of Lord Vishnu.

3. Shore Temple, Mahabalipuram—This wonderful temple of Lord Vishnu and Lord Shiva is situated in Mahabalipuram. Although this temple is dedicated to Boar incarnation of Lord Vishnu, yet it also has Lord Shiva's image in it.

4. Ranganath Swamy Temple, Tiruchirapalli—This temple complex is one of the largest in India. Lord Vishnu's shrine is situated on the Island of River Kalleri. The main temple is surrounded by seven enclosures and twenty-one entrances. A big festival called Vaikuntha Ekadashi is held here annually from November to December.

Lord Vishnu has a large number of devotees in India. He has thousand names. Some of them are: -

Prabhu	–	The Lord of all
Vidhata	–	The Creator of fruits and all deeds
Vikrami	–	Chivalrous
Shranam	–	The Shelter of all
Ahah	–	The Light form
Satyah	–	The Truth
Sahishnu	–	The Tolerant

Lord Shiva—The Destroyer

Lord Shiva is called the "Lord of Destruction" as he destroys the entire world when the negativity of the sins of people gets accumulated beyond extent, in the universe. The natural disasters like earthquakes and floods occur at public places, all due to the negativity of sins. The negativity of the sins can be removed by the chanting of God's names. If the negativity of the sins is not eliminated, the man has to suffer the outcome of his deeds; therefore Lord Shiva carries out destruction of the entire world, to grant punishments to the people engrossed in the world-play, with no control over their senses.

People who can't control anger and sexual urge, and become proud, and haughty, such people are Sinners. They are condemned by Almighty God and granted severe punishments for their sins. Supreme God has appointed "Lord Shiva" as the destroyer of the world. Lord Shiva is called Mahakala, Shankar, Mahadeva, Bhooteshwar, Augadh, Natraj, Yogiraj, Lingaraj, Pashupati and Rudra. The word "Rudra" signifies the forces of destruction, "Pashupati" means "the master of animal world", "Lingaraj" means "the personification of the eternal reproductive power of nature", "Natraj" is the King of Dance, "Yogiraj" means "the greatest ascetic", Augadh signifies the carefree revealer, "Mahakala" means "the Lord of Time".

The term "Shankar" symbolises the giver of happiness and prosperity, "Mahesh" means the "Grand Lord" and "Bhooteshwar" means the Lord of all Ghosts, Goblins and those spirits, who are no more in physical existence. According to the Hindu Scriptures, Lord Shiva destroys every thing by opening his third eye that is located in the midst of the forehead. Lord Shiva is simple, kind and innocent by nature. He gets aggressive and happy very quickly. He also grants boons to his devotees, who worship him in true faith.

Supreme God puts all the gods, goddesses and good human beings to a test. He wants to test whether the gods or human beings are worthy to be rewarded or not. Supreme God grants all the honour, wealth and powers to his most beloved children. But God wants to test his most gifted children whether, they are worthy of those rewards or not. Therefore he has made devils and other temptations to put his most beloved children into test. The Lord of Love was sent to tempt Lord Shiva, but Lord Shiva got aggressive, and burnt him with his third eye. The great gods like Lord Shiva are not tempted with these kinds of allurements. Lord Shiva is a multi-faceted personality of the spiritual world. Sometimes he performs wonderful dances and thus is called "the King of Dances". Lord Shiva's dance is called "Tandava" dance. This kind of dance represents annoyance and grief and thus is the dance of destruction. Other dance is "Lasya", that represents joy and peace. Lord Shiva had two wives– Sati and Parvati. In fact, Parvati was the re-incarnation of Sati. There is a legend behind the reincarnation of Sati as Parvati.

Sati was the devoted wife of Lord Shiva and loved him from the core of her heart. One day while visiting the holy places, she saw her husband, Lord Shiva bowing before "Lord Rama". Surprised at his deep regard for Lord Rama, she enquired her husband why did he bow before Rama when he was the most powerful of all gods. Lord Shiva replied that Lord Vishnu was more powerful than him and Lord Rama was the incarnation of Lord Vishnu. Sati still did not agree. She wanted to test Lord Rama. Thus she took the form of Lord Rama's wife Sita to know whether he recognised her in this form or not. Lord Rama immediately recognised that she was not his wife Sita but Goddess Sati. Since he was humble and knowledgeful, he respectfully bowed before her and asked that why she was roaming alone in the dense forest without her husband Lord Shankar. Goddess Sati left quickly without answering his questions. Now her doubts were cleared and she had realised that Lord Rama was indeed a divine entity on Earth.

When Sati reached home, Lord Shiva was lost in deep meditation, but somehow, he sensed about his wife's arrival. After coming back from the trance he enquired about the result of her test. She said that she accepted whatever he said. Though Sati did not tell him that how did she conduct the test, but Lord Shiva had come to know that Sati had taken the form of Sita to test Lord Rama. Since Sita was like a mother to Lord Shiva, he could not accept Sati as his wife any longer. Though he did not tell Sati about it openly, but, mentally severed relations with her. Sati was disappointed with her husband's behaviour, but she could not get an opportunity to plead her case before him, as he had already gone into a trance. Sati became sad because of her husband's indifferent attitude towards her.

One day, Sati's father Daksha arranged a spiritual party to celebrate his status of Prajapati. Sati sought her husband's permission to attend the sacrifice. Lord Shiva was initially reluctant to send her over there as he felt that Daksha had not invited them, therefore, it was not appropriate for them to attend the party uninvited, but finally had to give up when his wife refused to budge from her stand. Lord Shiva gave her the permission to attend the party arranged by her father.

When Sati reached the venue, nobody except her mother welcomed her. Her sisters and father showed her contempt. Sati felt insulted. As she proceeded towards the main hall where the sacrifice was taking place, she was shocked to find that oblations were offered to all gods and goddesses, except her husband. She came before the sacrificial fire, and prayed that she should be made Lord Shiva's consort in next birth too, thereafter she jumped into the pit of fire and ended her life.

Lord Shiva was deeply shocked when he heard about the death of his wife. He created a demon called Veerabhadra and appointed him the leader of his army of ghosts, goblins and hounds. Thereafter he gave orders to Veerabhadra to destroy Daksha immediately. Veerabhadra created more of his soldiers with the pores of his skin, went to Daksha's court, insulted the priests and eliminated Daksha by hacking of his head.

After that, Lord Shiva went there and took the body of his dead wife along with him. He was overwhelmed with sorrow and grief. He placed the body of his wife on his shoulders and went around the world for seven times in grief. Thereafter he sought solace in meditation.

As Sati had prayed before the holy-fire, to make her Shiva's wife in next birth too, her wish was fulfilled. She was born as Parvati who allured Lord Shiva with her sweet gestures of pure love.

Lord Shiva is one of the most adorable gods of Hindus. He is a carefree spiritual personality who gets angry and pleased very quickly. When angry, he becomes the cause of destruction, when pleased, he grants boons to his devotees. Lord Shiva loves the Berry of Rudra, which is called Rudraksha as per the Hindu Scriptures. Rudraksha is said to cure many diseases such as high blood pressure, neurological disorders and skin ailments. It is said that the Rudraksha wearer is abundantly blessed by Lord Shiva and his all desires are fulfilled, provided he wears it with faith.

Many temples have been built for the worship of Lord Shiva. Few of the temples are given below : –

1. Shree Kedarnath—This elegant shrine is built on Kedarnath, which is near Badrinath. It can be reached by traversing 12 to 14 kms. by foot or through ponies. It is believed to have been originally built by two ascetics Nara and Narayana who were the great devotees of Lord Shiva.

2. Shree Vishwanath—This magnificent temple is situated at Kashi, which is also called Varanasi. It is believed that Lord Shiva cut off Brahma's fifth head when Brahma declared himself supreme. The head of Brahma adhered to Shiva's hand and could not be shaken off. Lord Shiva tried every austerity but everything went in vain. Finally he came to Kashi and here the head instantly fell off. Therefore, this place became holy and gained popularity in the entire nation because of its purity and spiritual powers. It is said that whosoever dies in this place, goes in heaven.

3. Shree Omkareshwar—This is one of the most popular places of Madhya Pradesh. A big fair takes place on the occasion of Kartik Poornima. It is believed that Kubera, the Lord of Wealth, performed severe austerities for 100 years to please Lord Shiva.

4. Shree Vaidyanath Dham—According to the religious scriptures, the heart region of the Lord Shiva's wife Sati fell over here after Lord Shiva carried her dead body over his shoulders and Lord Vishnu hacked her dead body into pieces.

Lord Shiva is extremely loyal to his wife, a doting father and the great Lord, who bestows abundant blessings to all his devotees. Here is a prayer given to obtain his grace.

Na Janami Yogam Japam, naiva poojam,

Natoahm Sada Sarvada Shambhu tubhyam,

Jara Janma dukkough tatapyamanam,

Prabho Pahi Apannamanneesh Shambho.

Meaning: O Lord, O Shambho! O God! I neither know anything about Yoga nor penance nor about ritual worship. O Shambho! I always regard you in high esteem! Please redeem me from the afflictions of age decay and sorrow, and protect me by your grace.

Lord Krishna— The Lord of Lords

Gunakaram Sukkha Karam Kripa Karam Kripa Karam,

Suradwishannikandanam namami gopa nandanam,

Naveenagopa nagaaran naveenakelilampatam,

Namami Megha Sundram tadit prabhalasatpatam.

Meaning: To him I bow in reverence, the mine of all virtues, the ocean of happiness, the fountain of all grace and the compassionate Gopal, who is the destroyer of all enemies of the gods. To him I bow in reverence, who is eternally engrossed in his sportive love plays, the hued Gopal, the most exacted dancer wearing the yellow garment as bright as the flash of lightening.

Lord Krishna is one of the most popular spiritual entities of the entire world. He is known to have eliminated the demons like Kansa with his mighty strength and spiritual powers. Lord Krishna was the eighth son of Vasudeva and Devaki. Devaki was the cousin sister of Demon Kansa. After marriage, both of them were being driven in the chariot of Kansa, while Kansa was driving the chariot himself, out of extra-affection for his sister Devaki. All of a sudden, he heard a voice, "O Kansa! Your sister's eighth issue shall be the cause of your death." Kansa was red with rage after hearing these words. He decided to kill his cousin sister. But her husband Vasudeva requested him not to kill his wife, and promised that he shall deliver all issues one by one at his doorstep. Now Kansa thought of sparing Devaki on the condition that they would give each of their issue to Kansa so that he could kill them. Thereafter Kansa kept them in the prison so that he could get each of their issues at his doorstep. In due course of time, Devaki gave birth to seven male children, Kansa killed all of them mercilessly. Finally on the eighth lunar day of the month, Devaki gave birth to her eighth son. Since Lord Krishna was the eighth son of Devaki, an unusual happening took place on his birth. The doors of the prison opened up automatically and the guards went off to sleep. Vasudeva got an opportunity to take the newborn child across River Yamuna, to his friend Nanda's house. A divine voice prompted Vasudeva to exchange his son with the newly born daughter of Nanda. After crossing through all the obstacles and difficulties on the way, he finally exchanged his son with the newly born daughter of Nanda, and came back to the prison. The doors of the prison automatically closed and the guards on the duty woke back again. While Kansa was going to kill the newly born girl, a voice spoke, "O Rogue, your slayer has already taken birth". Kansa got so furious that he killed all the newly born children, but yet could not kill Krishna, as he was the Lord of all Lords.

Krishna began to grow up under the loving care and shelter of his parents Nanda and Yashoda. One day Kansa sent a demon called Putana to kill Krishna. Putana transformed into a graceful woman, and took the child on her knee to feed him. Krishna touched her breast that was full of poison and took out her life-air. Putana resumed her original self and died. Thereafter a demon called Shakatasur was sent to kill Krishna. Krishna was playing under a bullock-cart in the yard when the demon got into the cart with an intention to break it and kill Krishna, but Krishna knew what was in his mind. So he threw the cart on the other side of the yard and the demon was killed instantly. Kansa sent another demon named Vrittasur to kill Krishna. Vrittasur changed into a calf to befool Krishna. Krishna noticed this. He caught hold of the demon calf by the two hind-legs and tail, swung him around and threw him up towards the tree. Thereafter Kansa sent a demon called Bakasur, who transformed into a gigantic duck. The demon duck tried to kill him by pinching him with the beak, but Krishna caught hold of that beak and split the mouth. Gods in the heavens were greatly pleased by Krishna's mighty spiritual powers. They showered flowers from the skies. Besides this Krishna also killed many other demons including Demon Dhenukasura and Demon Pralambasur. Krishna was romantic and naughty by nature. He would hide the clothes of the girls who went to the river to take bath. Then he would play melodious tunes on the flute to enchant them. It was a way to attract the pure-hearted souls towards him.

Krishna also killed the deadly demon, Kansa with his mighty strength.

Krishna never utilised his strength, powers, position, and beauty for wrong purpose. He killed demons for the benefit of the mankind. He played pranks to make life interesting. He married girls who were betrayed by their husbands despite of their innocence. He attracted souls with pure love. Lord Krishna always took the side of the righteous people, overlooking their lack of physical strength, prestige and position in the society. For him "Law of God" was supreme before anything else. Lord Krishna became the charioteer of Pandavas, when they had to fight in the war to defend their rights from their cousin brother Duryodhana, who had snatched away their kingdom from them by wrong means. Lord Krishna taught many spiritual values to his disciple Arjuna, when Arjuna refused to fight against his near and dear ones in the war. Lord Krishna told him that he was also God. To attain him, one must remain in good spirits, and should not desire for anything in the world. He told him that one must do his best efforts in the right direction and should leave the rest on Almighty God.

God gives the rewards of his efforts. Besides that, he also told him not to renounce the world for God, one must work, but should never forget God while being engrossed in work. One must give priority to God before anything else in the world. Krishna gave abundant respect to all women. He never insulted any innocent woman. He never exploited any ignorant woman for his vested interest. He imparted knowledge to ignorant women to show them the right direction of life. Had he been born in this age, he would have taught lessons to all those men and women, who ill treat young innocent girls by finding faults in everything that they do and forcing them to work day and night to serve their husbands and in-laws. Lord Krishna would have also taught lessons to people who are misguiding ignorant girls, instead of giving right guidance to them. Lord Krishna might not be present in physical form among us today, but is always watching our deeds from the heavens, and all those men and women who ill treat ignorant people, beware of your deeds, as you are bound to be punished for your evil-deeds one day.

WORSHIP OF LORD KRISHNA & SHREE RADHA'S COMBINED ADOLESCENT IMAGE

Aarti Jugal Kishore ki keejai,

Tan Man-dhan Nyochhavar keejai,

Ravi-Shashi koti badan jaki shobha,

Gaur-Shyam mukha nirkhatreejhai,

Jugal Swaroop nayan bhar peejai,

Kanchan thâr kapoor kee batee,

Mari aye nirmal bhayee chhatee,

Phulam kee saf phulam vanmala,

Ratana Simhasana Paudhe Nanda Lala,

Mor-Mukut kar Maralee Sohe,

Natwar Vesha dekhi man Mohe,

Odhen neela-peeta-pat-saree,

Kunjaviharin Lala-Biharee,

Shree Purushottam giravaradharee,

Aarti Karat Sakal Vraj-naree,

Nanda-nandan vrikabhanu kishoree,

Paramananda Swami avichal joree.

Meaning: Come, let us move the lighted lamps round the adolescent couple image of Lord Krishna and his beloved Radha, that outshines the effulgence of millions of suns and moons, that is supremely mesmerising. Let our eyes be filled with the vision of the couple that captivates us even at the first sight. Let's bring a gold plate and place a lighted camphor wick and move the flame at their joint image, that would make the God remove all the filth from our hearts. Reposing upon the gem-embedded and flower cushioned bed, the son of Nanda and his beloved have flowery garland round their necks. Lord Krishna has a peacock-feather-diadem over his head and the flute in his hand; his flute player form is very mesmerising. Lord Krishna and his beloved are attired in yellow and blue remnants. The best among men, the lifter of the Mount Govardhan, the Son of Nanda, Krishna, and daughter of Brishabhan's (Radha's), this form is adored in the entire Vraj region. Paramananda Swami says that theirs is an immortal pair.

Lord Rama—The Divine Hero

Shantam Shashwatama prameya managham nivanran shaktipradam,

Brahma Shambhu phaneedrasevyamanisham vedant vedyam vibhum,

Ramakhyam Jagdeeshwaram Suragurm maya Manushyam Narim,

Vandeaham karunakaram Raghuvaran bhoopalachoodamanim.

Meaning: I adore him, who is the peaceful, eternal, beyond all means of cognition, who grants the peace of final liberation, whom Brahma, Shambhu and Serpent King always regard in high esteem, revealed by Vedanta, all pervading Lord of the World, preceptor of Gods appearing in human form through his mammon powers, the crest jewels of kings in whom all mercy dwells, prince of the house of Raghu who is famous by the name Rama.

Lord Rama took birth in the house of the reigning ruler of Ayodhya, King Dashrath. His mother's name was Kaushalya. Kaushalya was the eldest queen of Dashrath. Ram was born on the ninth lunar day of the bright fortnight of the Chaitra month, which is celebrated all over the nation as Ram Navmi today.

King Dashrath had three queens–Kaushalya, Kaikeyi and Sumitra. Kaushalya bigoted Ram, Kaikeyi–Bharat and Sumitra gave birth to twins–Lakshman and Shatrughan. Bharat and

Ram were dark-complexioned, but Lakshman and Shatrughan possessed very fair complexion. All the brothers loved each other from the core of their hearts.

One day, the great sage Vishwamitra came to King Dashrath's court and requested him to send his two sons Ram and Lakshman to his place, as he was performing worship in the spiritual fire, and wanted it to be protected from the demons, who always created obstacles in the Yajnas; with their demoniac powers. The King was initially reluctant to send his young sons over there, but observing the sage's temper, finally agreed. Ram and Lakshman obediently followed Sage Vishwamitra. On the way, they confronted powerful demons like Tadaka, Khara-Dooshan, Mareecha. All of them were defeated and killed by valiant Rama.

On the way, Lord Rama and his brother Lakshman saw a solitary hermitage, which consisted of the statue (stone-image) of Ahalya, who had become statue due to the curse of her sage-husband Gautama. She had had sex with the chief of Gods, Indra, considering him her husband when her husband had gone out. Indra had cheated her by taking the form of her husband. Sage Gautama, who was her husband cursed her to remain a statue and would only redeem her true self with the touch of Rama. Lord Rama touched the statue and Ahalya came to her original self. She went away glorifying Ram.

After that, they reached Sage Vishwamitra's hermitage and requested the sage to continue to perform sacrifice. While sage was performing sacrifice, numerous demons came to create obstacles in the spiritual fire, but Ram and Lakshman defeated them all and they had to run away to save their lives.

After that Lord Ram proceeded towards Mithila, where King Janak was holding a ceremony to choose suitable groom for his daughter "Sita".

He had invited princes from many kingdoms to attend the function. The girl's hand was supposed to be given to the person who was able to break Lord Shiva's mighty bow.

Ram and Lakshman reached the place where the function was being held. Many kings and princes had arrived to try their luck. None of them was able to break the bow. Finally Ram got up, in a moment lifted the bow and broke it. Janak was overwhelmed with joy. He arranged a formal marriage ceremony and got his daughter Sita married to Lord Rama. Rama was not only a faithful husband, but an obedient son, a doting father and above all a true human being who was true to his words and deeds. Lord Rama was sent to 14 years of exile by his stepmother Kaikeyi. Kaikeyi wanted that her son, Bharat should become the King of Ayodhya instead of Rama.

King Dashrath was shocked at her attitude, but Lord Ram obeyed her. In spite of the fact that she was being unjust to him, he did not protest against the wrongs. Lord Rama wanted to teach the moral values of obedience and regards towards the elders. If he would have not practiced these moral values himself, then how could he teach them. Therefore, he obeyed the word of his stepmother Kaikeyi, and went to 14 years of exile. Rama and Lakshman went towards the Godavari river and built a home over there for themselves.

One day, a female demon named Shoorpanakha, who was the sister of Demon Ravana, happened to see Rama. She fell in love with Ram instantly. She came towards Rama in a form of a beautiful damsel and proposed marriage to him. Rama pointed towards Sita and told her that he was already married. Both the brothers laughed at her silly behaviour. Shoorpanakha felt insulted and in order to take revenge from them, sent many demons to destroy them, but the two valiant brothers eliminated all of them. Thereafter she tempted her brother Ravana to abduct Sita to take her as his wife, as Sita was extremely beautiful to behold. Ravana was a notorious demon. He came into the talks of his sister and abducted Sita in the absence of Rama and Lakshman. Sita went on calling Rama but no one listened to her. Rama went with his army of monkeys to the battleground to kill Ravana and save innocent Sita from his clutches. Lord Hanuman, the chief of monkeys' army was always beside Rama to support him in his mission. Lord Hanuman was the most devoted disciple of Lord Rama. After reaching the battlefield, Rama valiantly fought with Ravana to eliminate him. Rama sent an arrow that hacked off Ravana's one head, but another grew in place of it. This way Rama hacked off Ravana's 10 heads. Finally, Vibhishan, Ravana's brother, told Rama that Ravana had a nectarous pit below his head that refused to allow life air escape through his body. Therefore, he ought to dry up that nectar by shooting a fiery arrow at his navel; only then, he could kill him. Rama acted on his wise advice and shot a weapon named "Brahma Weapon" at Ravana. The divine weapon sucked up the nectar in his body and Ravana was killed.

That was the end of foolish Demon Ravana. After the death of Ravana, his forces surrendered and Vibhishan was appointed as the King of Lanka. After the completion of 14 years, Lord Rama returned to Ayodhya along with Sita and Lakshman, where he was greeted with huge procession of horses, elephants and troops of soldiers.

Jai Saguna nirguna,

roop roop anoop bhoop siromane,

Daskan dharadi prachanda nisachar prabal khal bhujabal hane,

Avatar nar Sansar bhar vibhanji daruna dukh dahe,

Jai Pranatapal dayal prabhu samjukta sakti namamahe.

Meaning: Glory to the crest jewel of kings, of incomparable beauty, O personal and impersonal form of Lord Almighty! You have slain Ravana and all the other formidable powerful and evil demons, Glory to thee! Descending in the form of man's you have rid the world of its burden and burnt to ashes its tormenting woes! Glory to thee, the merciful lord, protector of the supplicant, Thee we adore together with they consort, the power of the powerful.

Goddess Durga—Mother of the Mankind

No mantram no yantram taddapi cha na jane stuti maho,

Na chavhanan dhyanam tadapi cha na jane stuti katha,

Na jane mudraste tadapi cha na jane vilapanam,

Param jane matastua danusaranam klesha haranam.

Meaning: O Mother! I neither know any incantation, nor any system of worship, nor I know how to sing orison, I also am not aware of the means of invocation and do not know the art of meditation, neither I am versed in your various forms, nor I know how to weep in distress, but one thing I know for certain that mere following you is capable of destroying of all sorts of distress.

Goddess Durga is one of the most powerful demigods of the world. The story of Goddess Durga's origin is given below.

In the olden times, there was a powerful demon named Mahisha, who wanted to become the Chief of Gods. Therefore, he removed Indra, Surya, Agni, Vayu, Yam, Chandra and other gods from their seats and became the Chief of Gods himself. All the gods were deprived from the divine pleasures; thus, they began to roam around on the Earth like ordinary beings. Finally they went to Lord Brahma, Lord Vishnu and Lord Shiva to find a solution for their problem. Seeing their pathetic condition Lord Brahma, Lord Vishnu and Lord Shiva created a great Goddess with the combined power of their aura.

Goddess Durga was directed to protect Gods from the Demons. Goddess Durga destroyed the entire troublesome demon leader such as Chamar, Andhak, and Mahishasur. The Gods were overjoyed after the elimination of demons. They sang melodious hymns in praise of the Goddess and sought the boon from her to come to their rescue, whenever they were in trouble. Goddess Durga blessed them and disappeared. Goddess Durga has many names. She's called Chamunda, as she killed two powerful demons–Chanda and Munda. She is called Tara due to her dark complexion, Shodashi, as she liked the innocence of a young girl of 16 years, Chandi–because she likes to eat fouls, goats, lions, tigers and rams.

Vidyavantam Yashawantam lakshmivantam janam kuru,

Roopam dehi jayam dehi yasho dehi dwisho jahi.

Meaning: Mother, kindly make your devotees intelligent renowned and rich. Grant them good form, victory, fame, and destroy their enemies, that are troubling them in the form of lust and anger.

Saraswati—The Goddess of Knowledge and Learning

Namah Saraswati roope namah savitri shankari,

Ganga Durga Sati Roope namo Lakshmi Swaroopini,

Mool Prakriti roopam twam bhajamah Karunaarvranam,

Sanskar Sagarat Asman Uddharand dayam kuru.

Meaning: O divine spirit, Bhagawati in the form of Saraswati, Savitri, Shiva, Ganga, Durga, Sati and Lakshmi, accept our repeated and devoted salutations. O Ocean of Kindness, the Goddess of Nature in its pristine form, redeem us and take us across the sea of mundane existence.

Goddess Saraswati is the demigod of knowledge and learning. This great goddess originated from Lord Brahma's head hence was related to him by birth. She was the daughter of Lord Brahma. But Lord Brahma developed physical relations with her in ignorance. He possessed profound knowledge of many things, but was ignorant of the fact that one should not develop relations with one's own daughter. He was so ignorant about the father/daughter relationship that he even refused to accept the truth that Lord Vishnu was his father, when Lord Vishnu told him that since he has come out of his body, he was his son. Lord Brahma began to fight with Lord Vishnu, as he was ignorant about the relationship of father with their children. In ignorance, he committed adultery with his own daughter Saraswati.

The worship of Saraswati can make the most insane person of the world, sensible. It can miraculously change one's life. I shall narrate a real-life story of Goddess Saraswati's blessings upon a mad girl. Only a few years back, we were staying in Pandav Nagar. A muslim woman came to work for us. She used to do our household chores. She had two girls. One of them was normal, but the other was abnormal. Her senses were out of control. She was mad. All the three women loved me very much. I used to give them a little money here and there to keep them happy. Besides salary, they were given extra facilities too by our family. The mad girl never used to listen to others, but always obeyed me, as I dealt her psychologically. One day, I gave the mad girl's mother a locket which had Goddess Saraswati's picture and divine symbols known as "Tantra" in Hindu Scriptures. I kept the Saraswati necklace on my third eye and prayed her to kindly bring the girl back to senses, as soon as possible. I gave the necklace to her mother. At first, she was reluctant to give the necklace to her daughter, as she was a muslim, but later on when I told her that she could continue to worship God in her own ways, but must make the girl wear the necklace of Goddess of Learning, for her own good. She agreed and took the necklace along with her. After a few days, she told me, that the girl has become so sensible that she wakes up everyday at sharp 4'o clock, takes a bath, gets ready and completes her entire work in no time. The girl who had no sense of timing, punctuality and hard work, had become extremely punctual and hard working with the grace of Goddess Saraswati.

Goddess Saraswati is extremely compassionate by nature. She bestows her blessings to those devotees, who have faith in her. Although one can worship her on any day to get her blessings, but Vasant Panchami (15th Jan to 15th Feb) is held to be the special day of worship of this elegant Goddess. The worship of Goddess is so significant that every mad man can gain sanity of mind, if his relatives pray to her with faith.

Chaturbhyam Chandravarnam Chaturanan Vallabham

Avahyam Vag-Devim Veena-Pustak dharineem.

Meaning: O Four armed, moon-complexioned beloved of the creator, I invoke thee, O Goddess of Speech, holding the lute and the book.

Goddess Ganga—An Epitome of Purity

In the olden times, there lived a king named Shantanu. He had a wide empire, but was ignorant of some facts of life. He was ignorant of the fact that one should not kill innocent and harmless animals. He would often go for hunting out of ignorance. One day, he was moving on the bank of River Ganga in the search of his prey when he saw a beautiful damsel sitting on the bank. Shantanu was mesmerized by the damsel's beauty. He proposed marriage to the girl, but the girl told him that the proposal was acceptable to her, but at some conditions. The conditions were that he would in no way try to identify her and she would be free to do whatever she likes. King Shantanu was greatly allured by her charms; therefore he agreed all her conditions, willingly. Soon both of them were married and they began to lead a happy blissful marriage. Everything was well and fine till, one day the woman became pregnant.

After giving birth to the child, she drowned him into the river. The king was hurt, but he didn't say anything as he was bound by his conditions. The lady kept on drowning her every child until King Shantanu stopped her when she was going to throw her eighth child. This time King Shantanu could not resist himself and he sternly told her that she could not dare to cause damage to his son this time, although, she could leave him, if she wanted to. Then the woman told him the reason, why she was drowning all their children one by one in the river. She told the given story: —

In the ancient times, there were eight Vasus. The Vasus are known to be the divine entities, which rule over the material wealth. One day, the wife of the eighth Vasu told him to steal a cow of the Sage Vashishtha. All of the brothers tried to resist her from stealing the cow as the cow was the property of the sage, but still she didn't agree. At last, they stole away the cow of the sage. When the sage learnt about the theft, he was red with rage. He cursed the eight Vasus that they would have to take birth in the mortal world. The Seven Vasus begged the sage to forgive them and not to punish them for the fault of the wife of the eighth Vasu. The sage developed a trifle compassion for them and modified his curse. He thereafter said that although the first seven Vasus would come back to their divine realm the moment they took birth in the mortal world, but the eighth Vasu shall have to dwell on the world, the longest period of time, and has to live additionally on the behalf of his brothers, who had departed from mortal world before him and shall also be deprived of the company of a female. Since these Vasus were noble souls, they could not descend into this mortal world through the womb of an ordinary woman, hence, the sage chose me to transform into a young woman and give birth to them. I am holy River Ganga.

After completing her story, holy River Ganga disappeared with her eighth son. After some years Ganga returned the eighth son back to Shantanu and told him that his son was extremely knowledgeful and wise, and his intelligence was up to the level of perfection. His name was Devrath. Thereafter Ganga disappeared. Holy River Ganga is known all over India for its piety and divine powers to cure many diseases. Innumerable people wash away their sins in this nectar.

Tava Jal mamalam yen nipeetam parampadam khalu tengriheetam,

Matargnage tvayi yo bhatah kilatam drashtum na yamah shaktah.

Meaning: O Goddess! He who drinks your pious water attains to the highest status–there is no doubt about it. He who is devoted to you is beyond the reach of God of Death, as all your devotees go to Baikunth realm and not the realm of death, when they quit their mortal frames.

Goddess Lakshmi—Demigod of Wealth and Prosperity

Goddess Lakshmi is one of the most popular spiritual deities of Hindus. She is the demigod of wealth and prosperity. She is believed to bestow abundant blessings on the auspicious occasion of Diwali festival. On this occasion, people lit up candles to invite Goddess Lakshmi in their homes. They clean up every part of dust to please their esteemed Goddess Lakshmi. On this day, old women are given preference to worship goddess. There is a story associated behind it. The story is given below: —

Once upon a time, there lived a king named Yashobarman in Manipur. He was a wise person, who respected wise people. His wife was also very pure hearted lady. She had a precious necklace worth nine lakhs of rupees, which was very dear to her. One day, she went to take a bath and kept the precious necklace on the rooftop, where a bird located it and flew away holding it in the beak. After coming from bathroom, the queen was shocked to find her necklace missing. She thought that some thieves have stolen the necklace. Thereafter she told the king about the missing necklace. The king sent his soldiers to find the missing necklace, but their entire search went in vain. They were not able to locate the queen's necklace, in spite of working hard to get it.

The kite that had taken the queen's necklace dropped it down near an old woman's hut. The old woman came to realise that it belonged to the queen, therefore planned to return it back to the queen, as she was afraid of being caught as a thief.

Thereafter she thought of returning the necklace back to the king, with the condition, that he would promise to give a handsome reward that would grant her eternal prosperity.

Thereafter she proceeded towards the capital. Thereafter she returned the necklace to the king. The king returned it back to the queen. The queen and king were both very delighted after getting the lost necklace back. The king asked the old woman, what she wanted to as reward? The old woman retorted back that she wanted to have the sole right of worshipping Goddess Lakshmi on the Diwali Day and didn't want any one else to worship her as she felt that if others also worship Goddess on that day, her blessings would be divided, and her share would be much less. Hearing that the king asked her, whether she would allow him to worship her. Thereafter the old woman gave permission to everyone to worship goddess, on the condition that everyone else would worship goddess only after she has finished worshipping her. The king agreed.

From then onwards every old woman is given first right to worship Goddess Lakshmi.

Goddess Lakshmi is believed to be the wife of Lord Vishnu. Lakshmi can be worshipped in a very simple way. Just offer this prayer to Mother Lakshmi daily "O Goddess Lakshmi, you are the bestower of wealth and materialistic comforts of life. Kindly grant me abundant wealth to keep my family and myself happy, throughout our life."

This simple prayer should be offered daily with full concentration in the middle of your eyebrows. This prayer can bring miraculous prosperity in your life, on the condition that you offer this prayer with faith to the goddess everyday.

A person can also attain blessings of Goddess Lakshmi by visiting her temples once in a week. Some of her temples are given below: —

1. Lakshmi Narayana Temple, Delhi—This temple was built by the Birlas in 1938. It is situated in Connaught Place. The temple envelops in beauty on Diwali days.

2. Lakshmi Narayana Temple, Jaipur—This magnificent temple is situated in the city of Jaipur near Moti Doongari. It is surrounded in the midst of lush green lawns and is made up of curvilinear marble.

3. Mahalakshmi Temple, Bombay—This elegant shrine is dedicated to Goddess Lakshmi. It is situated down the Malabar Hill. The Goddess is portrayed sitting with Lord Vishnu on the divine eagle named Garuda. Goddess Lakshmi is one of the most revered goddesses of Hindus. People sing her glories to get her esteemed self's blessings. Here is one prayer given to glorify Goddess Lakshmi and attain her blessings.

Aarti of Goddess Lakshmi

Jai Lakshmi Mata, Maiyya Jai Lakshmi Mata,

Tumko Nisdin sevat, Hara, Hari, au dhata,

Jai Lakshmi Mata!

Brahmani, Rudrani,Kamala tu hee jagmata,

Surya chandrama dhyavat, Naraaad Rishi gata,

Jai Lakshmi Mata!

Tero roop nirantar sukh sampati data,

Jo koi tumko dhyavat, dhansiddi pata,

Jai Lakshmi Mata!

Jis ghar mein tu rehati, sab sadgun aata,

Kar ne sake Jo kar leyi, man nahin Ghabrata,

Jai Lakshmi Mata!

Tum bin yagya no hove, Vastra na koi pata,

Khan pan ka vaibhava tum hee se ata,

Jai Lakshmi Mata,

Shubha gun Mandir sundar, ksheerdadhhhijata,

Ratna chaturdash tumheen, koi nahin pata,

Jai Lakshmi Mata!

Arti Lakshmi jee kee jo koi nar gata,

Ur ananda umagrati, pap utar jata,

Jai Lakshmi Mata!

Meaning: O Mother Lakshmi, victory to thee, victory to thee, even Shiva, Vishnu and Brahma glorify you day and night. Victory to thee, Mother Lakshmi, you are the mother of the world and you are also famous as Rudrani, Brahmani and Kamala. Even all luminaries like the Sun and Moon ever worship you with utmost devotion, and Sage Narad ever sings your glory. The devoted worship of your esteemed self certainly bestows all kinds of riches and happenings and he who worships you with full faith in his heart gets the desired boon and attains perfection. O Mother Goddess! All virtues are attracted to the house you dwell in and by your grace one accomplishes even that mission who's very thought gives one fright. Without your grace, it is impossible to accomplish any Yajna or big mission or get any prosperity, all affluence and even sensual pleasures depend upon your grace only. O daughter of the ocean of milk! You are the mine of all virtues. It was only your grace that enabled the gods to churn out the fourteen gems. Victory to thee, Mother Lakshmi. One who sings this aarti with total faith and devotion gets bliss in his heart and peace in his mind as all his sins get destroyed automatically. Victory to thee, Mother Lakshmi! Victory to thee!

Ganesh—
The Mighty of Wisdom and Success

Gaiye Ganapati Jag-Vandan,
Sankar-Suvan Bhavani nandan,
Gaiye Ganapati Jag-Vandan,
Siddhi Sadan Gaj-Vandan Vinayak,
Kripa-Sindhu Sundar Sab layak,
Modak priya mud-mangal data,
Vidya-Varidhi buddhi vidhata,
Mangat Tulsidas kar jore,
Basen Ram-Siya Manas More.

Meaning: Come; let us sing the virtues of Ganpati whom the whole world worships. He is the son of Lord Shankar and Bhavani, the home of Siddhi. This elephant-faced great leader loves laddoos and he bestows happiness and success to all. He is the treasure of knowledge and the god of wisdom. I pray him hand bound to make Lord Ram and Sita ever dwell in my heart.

Lord Ganesh is the demigod of wisdom and success. He eliminates the hurdles in the life of his devotees and grants them abundant success. His idol is kept in the offices and homes, to eliminate difficulties of life.

There is a story behind the birth of Lord Ganesh. The story is given below: —

One day Parvati, the wife of Lord Shiva, created a boy out of her own filth and scurf. Thereafter she directed him to guard the gate, while she took bath. The boy was very handsome and intelligent. He was extremely attractive. One day, Lord Shiva rushed towards his wife's chambers while she was taking a bath. The boy stopped him to proceed inside. Lord Shiva got furious and again told the boy to get aside as he was the husband of Goddess Parvati. The boy was firm in his decision. He refused to let him in. Lord Shiva became furious. He ordered his servants to tell the boy, who he was. His servants tried their best to let him in but the boy did not budge from his stand. Finally the henchman began to fight with boy, but the mighty boy gave such severe blows to them that they had to run for their lives. After that Lord Brahma came to change his mind, but the naughty boy plucked his flowing beard, causing him injury. After that Lord Shiva and Lord Vishnu came with a huge force to teach him a lesson, but the valiant boy defeated them all. Now Lord Shiva was red with rage. He hacked off the boy's trunk. It went off with a thunderous sound. The sound was so powerful that Mother Parvati came rushing to see her son beheaded. She was so disappointed with her son's death, that she created a hundred thousand deadly powers and directed them to devour all the celestial power that had killed her son. Finally Narad began to sing her glories to calm her. After a long period, she became somewhat calm. Narad pleaded, "O Goddess, your son was indeed the mightiest of all gods and demons. We are extremely sorry at his death. What should we do to attain your love back?" "Well, you can get that only on one condition. Revive my son back to life and declare him to be the foremost God among all the celestials."

The condition of reviving him back to life was accepted. Thereafter an elephant's head was planted on his headless body. The elephant was the only creature at that time, which had been born at the same day and at the same time.

Lord Ganesh is an innocent and benevolent demigod of the world. He showers his blessings to each and every person, who remembers him with faith.

Lord Ganesh has many names. He is called "Ganpati" which means "Chief of Lord Shiva's henchmen", the name "Umaputra" means "the son of Uma or Parvati" and Sarva-Siddhanta means "one who is capable of making everything possible".

Prayer to Lord Ganesh

Jai Ganesh, Jai Ganesh, Jai Ganesh Deva,

Mata Jaki Parvati, Pita Mahadeva,

Ekdant Dayavant Charbhuja dhari,

Mathe Sindoor Sohe, moosey ki savari,

Andhan ko Ankha deta, kodhin ko kaya,

Banjhan ko putra deta, nirdhan ko maya,

Pan chadhe phool chadhe aur chadhe meva,

Laddun ka bhog lage, sant Karen Seva.

Meaning: He, whose mother is Parvati and father Mahadeva, I hail Lord Ganesh repeatedly. He, who is one tusked and kind, who has four arms and his forehead, is gracefully marked with Vermillion powder and whose vehicle is a mouse.

By worshipping whom the blind get their eyes, the lepers get beautiful physique, the barren women get sons and the paupers come in riches.

He who is worshipped with betel leaves, flowers, rich dry fruits and delicious laddoos (sweets), who is ever serviced by the nobles and sages, may such lord be gracious to me.

Shankaracharya—The Great Master

Gurucharanambuja nirbhar bhaktah,

Sansaradachiradbhva Muktah,

Sendriyamana Shiyama devam dakshyasi,

Nijahridayastham devam,

Dwadashapanjari Kamaya eshah Shishyanam kathi to hyupdeshah,

Yesham chitte naiva vivekastey pachyantey narkamanekam.

Translation: Be a dedicated devotee to your Guru's Lotus like feet and liberate yourself from the world soon! Thus withdrawing all your senses from external objects and concentrating them into your internal self, you will soon see the divine spirit reposing on your heart, hence always keep on chanting the name of Govinda (God). For whom, who lack this wisdom, languish in hell suffering all kinds of tortures. Hence O Fool! Ever chant the name of Govinda-Shankaracharya

Shankaracharya was one of the most profound thinkers of the world. He was an ocean of virtues like compassion, divinity, spiritualism and love. This great soul took birth in the home of learned couple Shivguru and Aryamba, on the fifth day of the bright half of the lunar month Vaisakh in 788 A.D. Shankar was a brilliant child from his very childhood. At the age of one, he learnt Sanskrit, at two, he could read books and at three he could understand Kavyas and Puranas.

Unfortunately, Shankar lost his father at a very young age. Yet, he didn't accept defeat in life and shouldered the responsibilities of life with great courage and determination. He was sent to a formal school for the study of the Vedas and other branches of knowledge. He would surpass all other students in his mental ability to grasp things. What others would learn in twenty years, he would learn within two years. In a short time, he achieved mastery over the scriptural text such as Puranas, Upanishads and Dharmashastra, Nyaya (Jurisprudence) and Sankhya Yoga (Mathematics and Logic). In spite of being a great scholar, Shankaracharya was down-to-earth, humble person, who didn't crave for materialistic possessions of life, and neither was proud of his academic accomplishments, therefore, to keep himself humble he lived by begging. He would sometimes utter miraculous prayers for good souls.

One day he visited the house of a poor woman. The woman was poor but kind. She didn't have anything else to give him in alms except a stale myrobalam fruit. She gave that to him. Shankaracharya was overwhelmed with pity at the pathetic condition of the poor family. He uttered a prayer to Goddess Lakshmi to bless the poor woman with wealth, and surprisingly his prayers were answered immediately. The Goddess did bless the woman with abundant wealth of gold.

Shankaracharya gained popularity far and wide, with his miraculous prayers and virtuous deeds. The King of Kerela was so much allured by the boy's charms, that he sent his minister to invite the boy in his palace, but the great master refused to come, as he had no desire for materialistic possessions, status and prestige. He was only inclined to serve God and his men with virtuous deeds. When the little master refused to come to the court of the king, then the devout king himself came to Kaladi to meet the boy.

The little master gained immense powers with meditation and chanting of holy names of god. Once his mother became unconscious due to the scorching heat. Shankaracharya sprinkled holy water on her face and revived her. Shankaracharya never used his spiritual powers for personal gains. He used them for the welfare of innocent souls, at the time of their need.

Shankaracharya believed that one should not only love one's own family members, but the entire world, because God's light prevails in each and every living and non-living thing in the world.

Shankaracharya wanted to propagate his religion of love in the entire world. He visited many places within a short period of time, and taught men the principles of love towards god and his creations. While on his stay in Nepal, the Acharya visited Kedarnath and installed Mulkti Linga. Besides that visited places like Puri, Trichurapura, Kashi, Chidambaram etc. and established many temples for the benefit of people, suffering from various ailments, turmoils and difficulties of life.

Shankaracharya was a true saint by his words and deeds. He practiced all that he taught. Some of his preachings are given below: —

1. *Tvayi mayi chanyo treiko,*

   Vishuvyartham Kupyasi Sarvasahishnuh!

   Sarvasi mannapi pashyatmanam,

   Sarvatrotsray bhedagyanam Bhaj.

Translation: For the same Lord Vasudeva dwells in you and me and in each and every thing prevalent in the universe, therefore it is futile to develop enmity with anyone, as all are instinct with the same spirit. Be tolerant and know that divine spirit prevails in every one. Shed your ignorance that makes you see the differences and ever chant the name of Govinda.

2. *Pranayamam Pratyaharam nityanitya viveka Vicharam!*

   Japyasameta samadhi vidhanan karvadhanam mahadeva dhanam.

Translation: Exercising breath control and having withdrawn the senses from external objects, and discerning what is eternal and what is transitory, make resolve of religiously worshipping Lord Almighty because this is the sole true determination in the mortal world. Ever chant the Govinda's name.

3. *Makuru dhanafana yauvan garvam,*

Harati nimeshat kalahsarvam,

Maya Maya Midamakhilam hitva,

Brahmapadam tvam pravisha viditva.

Translation: Never be proud of money, worldly benefits or youth since time can destroy all of them in a trice! Leave all these illusions, realise Supreme Being and surrender yourself into him! And ever chant the name of Govinda.

Brahma Purana

The Puranas are the sacred texts of Hindus that consist the stories of the demons, devils, gods, goddesses, human beings and other living beings. Every story has a meaning. They portray the creation of god, the victory of truth over falsehood and the plight of the weak people, who were exploited by strong for vested interest. They also portray, how the creation of the world took place and how it expanded.

The Puranas are divided into many parts such as the Brahma Purana, Vishnu Purana, Shiva Purana, Vayu Purana and so on. To understand them thoroughly let's begin with Brahma Purana.

The Brahma Purana states how the world was created, and how it was expanded. Initially, there was water everywhere. Lord Vishnu slept on the bed of water and there emerged a golden egg. Lord Brahma was born inside the egg. Lord Brahma lived in the egg for one whole year and thereafter split the egg into parts and created heaven and Earth. After that created skies, time, direction, senses and language in both Heaven and Earth. Thereafter to expand his creation further, Brahma gave birth to a man called SVAYAMBHUVA MANU and the woman named Shatarupa. They had many descendants. This was how the world expanded. Brahma Purana consists of many stories of God's creation, operation and destruction. One of them is based on a sage called Markandeya.

One day Sage Markandeya was busy meditating on God, when a great destruction took place. The whole world was enveloped with darkness. There was neither Sun nor Moon. Lakes and rivers dried up and the entire Earth burnt with flaming fire. Since Markandeya was busy meditating on God, the fire could not harm him. But the sage got fearful. He suffered from hunger and thirst. His lips and throat dried up out of fear. But somehow he got relief when he saw a Banyan tree, which was untouched by these disasters. He sat under the shade of the Banyan tree and began to pray to Lord Vishnu. Dark clouds spread all over the Earth and brought abundant rain. The water put out the fire. It rained continuously for twelve years. Markandeya began to float on the water, but continued to pray to Lord Vishnu. Thereafter Vishnu came to him and said that he ought not to be frightened as he was by his side.

Markandeya could not realize who was talking to him. He didn't know from where the voice has come. All of a sudden, he saw a banyan tree floating on the water. A golden bed was spread on the branches of the tree, a small boy slept on the bed. Markandeya was astonished to see the little boy floating on the water. In a perplexed mind, he wondered who was he. The boy told Markandeya that he should enter his body, as he was tired. Confused Markandeya entered the boy's body through his mouth and discovered all the worlds, the seven regions, the seven oceans, the mountains, living creatures and everything else prevalent in the world.

Markandeya was confused. He again began to pray to Lord Vishnu. Thereafter he came out of the boy's mouth. Now Vishnu appeared before him and showered abundant blessings upon him. The sage spent thousand years with Lord Vishnu. Lord Vishnu was greatly pleased by the sage's devotion. He asked him if he had any desire that he wished to be fulfilled. Markandeya told him that he wanted to build a temple to Shiva in Purushottamkshetra. Vishnu granted the boon and Markandeya built a temple devoted to Lord Shiva known as "Bhuvaneshwar" (Lord of the World). Another story mentioned in Brahma Purana is about powerful King Vali.

Vali was an extremely powerful king. He was not only powerful but noble too. During his reign all the diseases, natural disasters and evils disappeared from the three worlds.

The demigods became jealous of his popularity. They approached Lord Vishnu and told him that they were not happy under the rule of Vali. Vishnu was though not pleased with their attitude towards Vali; yet, he didn't want to annoy them. Therefore he said that since Vali was his devotee, he could not fight with him, but could certainly find out a way so that his kingdom could be snatched from him and given to them.

Therefore Vishnu decided to be born as Dwarf in the house of Aditi.

One day, Vali organised a horse sacrifice. Many sages came to the sacrifice, out of them Shukracharya was the chief priest. The Dwarf also arrived. The head priest, Shukracharya came to realise that the Dwarf was the incarnation of Lord Vishnu. He told Vali not to grant any boon to Dwarf without consulting him. Vali did not agree. He said that since Lord Vishnu had come to his place, he would grant him, whatever he wanted.

Vali asked the Dwarf what did he want. Lord Dwarf replied that he might be given land that covers three of his steps. Vali immediately agreed to grant him the boon.

Now the Dwarf adopted a huge form. He placed one of his foot on Vali's Yajna and the second on Brahmalok. Thereafter he asked Vali that where should he place his third step. Vali replied that he should place it on his back. Vishnu was extremely pleased with Vali's humility. He gave abundant blessings to him and disappeared.

There is another story about the kind-hearted doves, mentioned in Purana. In the olden times, there lived a hunter who was very cruel and heartless. He not only killed birds and animals but Sages and Brahmans too.

Once the hunter went as usual for hunting in the forests. It became night and began to rain. The hunter lost his way. He climbed up a tree and decided to spend the night there. On the same tree, lived a dove and its family. Both the male and female had gone in search of food but unfortunately, the female had been caught by the hunter on its way back to home, whereas the male dove had returned back. The male dove didn't know that the female had been caught by the hunter. He thought that she had died on her way back home. He began to mourn for his wife. His wife heard his mourning. She called him up near the cage. The male dove saw the hunter sleeping, therefore, he wished to set his wife free, but his wife forbid him to do that as she felt that a living being lived on another living being, therefore since the hunter hunted for his meals, he was not wrong in doing such an act. Moreover he was their guest and it was their duty to offer their bodies to him. The male dove agreed with his wife.

But he wondered how to serve their guest. The female dove prompted him to lit up a fire to warm their guest. The male dove brought a flaming branch and many dry leaves and branches so that the fire could burn. The rain had already stopped when he lit up the fire for his guest.

After that, the dove told her husband to set her free so that she could immolate herself in the fire, so that her roasted flesh could serve as food for the hunter. But her husband told her that it was his right to serve their guest first, therefore, he hurled himself in the fire. After her husband's death, the female dove requested the hunter to set her free, once he set her free, she hurled herself in the fire and died. Meanwhile the hunter had heard their conversation. He was surprised at the selfless acts of the doves.

A magnificent space vehicle arrived to take the doves to heaven. The cruel hunter now repented for his past misdeeds. He spoke to the doves that before proceeding towards heaven they should tell him how to perform penance for his sins. The doves told him to go to Gautami Ganga for fifteen days if he wanted his sins to be forgiven. The hunter did as they directed him to do. His all sins were washed away by the holy water of River Ganga. The place where the doves immolated themselves became a holy spot known as Kapotatirtha. The word "Kapota" means dove. Therefore "Kapotatirtha" means "the holy spot of doves." This story portrays the sacrifice of the two doves for their guest hunters.

These were only few stories of the Brahma Purana. The Brahma Purana consists of many more such wonderful stories portraying the significance of repentance for one's own sins and the triumph of truth over falsehood. All these stories teach us to tread on the righteousness path and lead others on the path of truth.

Vishnu Purana

The Vishnu Purana throws light on many religious issues and contains religious scriptures that consist knowledgeful stories and philosophies. It has also mentioned a part of Astronomy. It states that the world of gods lies below the Brahma Lok (Abode of Brahma) and Vaikunthalok (Abode of Vishnu).

The Almighty God dwells at the highest abode and takes care of all the material and spiritual worlds situated below his abode.

Like heavens, god has created many hells. The Brahmans who eat cats, hens, goats go to a hell known as Rudhirandha, some Sinners are born as trees, worms, fishes, animals etc. Those who criticize good human beings go to a separate hell; those who ill-treat their daughters and daughters-in-law go to a separate hell and so on. After the death, the non-worshippers of god, come under the control of Lord Yama, the Administrator of Justice, appointed by Lord Vishnu.

The Sinners have to suffer punishments for their sins in the hells. After they have atoned for their sins, they are reborn in the mortal world in the form of a tree, bird, animal, human being etc.

The worshippers of god are not touched by Lord Yama. They enjoy the blissful union with god. Vishnu Purana has emphasised on the virtues of cleanliness, truthfulness, compassion and hard work.

According to the Hindu rituals, a person must not be envious of other's wealth and property. He should not compete with others, neither allow his children to get tempted to the temptations of life. He should also give ample respect to all the religious places and bow before the idols of gods and goddesses. The people are forbidden to hurt others by speech or by deed. There are severe punishments in store for the Sinners.

The story of Prahlada is described in a marvellous manner in Puranas. His story portrays the strength of God's name. God's name can even destroy the most powerful of all enemies within a fraction of a second.

Prahlada was the son of powerful King Hiranyakshapu. Hiranyakshapu was an extremely proud and selfish king. He had conquered three worlds, as per the boon granted by Lord Brahma. He wanted everyone to worship him.

Prahlada was sent away to study with his teacher. In the vacations, when he arrived home with his teacher, Hiranyakshapu wanted to know what his son has learnt from his teacher. "Well, I have learnt to pray to Lord Vishnu", Prahlada retorted back bluntly.

Hiranyakshapu was extremely angry at his truthful reply. "Who taught you this kind of non-sense?" he asked angrily. "None other than my Lord Vishnu, who is the creator of entire world including you" said Little Prahlada.

Hiranyakshapu was furious. "How dare you say like that? I am more powerful than Vishnu. You go and study further and realise that I am all powerful." said he to his son.

Prahlada went to his teacher's house and studied further for some more years. He was again brought back to Hiranyakshapu.

Again he asked his son what had he studied and again came the same reply "To pray to Lord Vishnu". Hiranyakshapu was so angry that he ordered his army soldiers to kill him. Many thousands of army soldiers attacked Prahlada with all sorts of weapons, but since Prahlada was protected by Lord

Vishnu, nothing could harm him. After that Hiranyakshapu let loose many poisonous snakes on Prahlada but with the grace of Lord Vishnu, nothing could harm him. Thereafter the furious king gave orders to release elephants to give him to death. Still nothing could harm him with the blessing of Lord Vishnu. Prahlada was put on fire but the flames could yet not harm him.

After that Hiranyakshapu did many efforts to kill him. Sometimes, he instructed his cooks to poison Prahlada's food sometimes threw him down from the top of the palace, sometimes kicked him on his chest, sometimes threw him in the midst of the snakes, yet, Prahlad survived all those attempts to end his life, due to the grace of Lord Vishnu.

Finally, Lord Vishnu himself took the form of the Man-Lion and killed Hiranyakshapu.

This story gives us a moral lesson that a proud man can even kill his own kiths and kins due to his inflated "Ego", and his own end is even worse than them, due to his misdeeds; therefore the man must keep "Pride" at bay. Another lesson that we draw from this story is that the worshipper of God has nothing to fear in the world, as he is always protected by him.

Shiva Purana

A beautiful damsel called Parvati had fallen in love with Lord Shiva. Parvati was in fact the incarnation of Shiva's first wife Sati, who had committed suicide due to depression.

Parvati didn't know how to meet Shiva and tell him about her feelings for him. One day a sage called Narad came and told her, "Lord Shiva is only pleased with meditation, the continous practice of meditation. Therefore, do meditation".

Parvati agreed to meditate on Lord Shiva, in order to attain him. She gave up her jewellery and beautiful clothes, instead wore deerskin, and went to the Himalayas to meditate on her dear god. In the monsoons, Parvati meditated on the ground, while in the winters, she meditated in water. Such was her aura that no animal dared to touch her. Even the gods, demigods and sages arrived to observe her wonderful ways of meditation. The gods and sages were deeply pleased by her meditation. "Lord" they prayed to Lord Shiva, "She is indeed a precious jewel. None has meditated like her before; none would meditate like her in future. Kindly fulfil her mind's desires."

Lord Shiva adopted the form of an old Brahman and appeared at Parvati's hermitage. Parvati gave ample regards to the Brahman and worshipped him with fruits and flowers. The Brahman asked her the reason for her continous practice of meditation. Parvati replied that she intended to have Lord Shiva as her husband. The Brahman forbid her from marrying Shiva attributing that Shiva was a stupid fellow, as his hair remained matted, and bodies were smeared with ashes, besides this, was accompanied by ghosts, therefore it was appropriate for her to leave the mad fellow and marry someone else. The Brahman's words angered Parvati. She called the Brahmin stupid for saying such words about the lord of everything and proceeded ahead to leave that place, immediately before he could further utter something nasty about Lord Shiva. Now Lord Shiva came to his original self. He was extremely pleased by Parvati's devotion towards him. He asked her for a boon. She told him to marry her according to the prescribed rites.

Shiva agreed for the same and Parvati returned back home.

Shiva sent of sages as messengers to King Himalaya's place seeking his daughter Parvati's hand for marriage. Himalaya was delighted by the marriage proposal sent by the great lord of the universe.

Finally, the auspicious occasion of the marriage arrived.

The singers sang melodious songs and the dancers danced. Himalaya built many gates in front of his house and placed flags on them.

When the procession arrived at the residence, Parvati's mother, Maneka rushed out to welcome them. She wanted to have a glimpse of Lord Shiva to observe how he looked like. She thought he would be very handsome, but she was extremely disappointed to see him in a wild form. Lord Shiva had arrived with the army of ghosts, who looked fierce with their dark complexion and dangerous appearances. Lord Shiva rode on a bull. He possessed three eyes five faces and ten arms.

Maneka was deeply shocked by his appearance. She fainted. After coming into her senses she chided Himalaya, Narad and Parvati for their misfortune. She told them that she would rather kill herself and her daughter than to get her married to Shiva. She would not allow her at any cost to get married to Shiva.

Lord Vishnu tried to pacify Maneka, but she did not agree. Finally Narad asked Shiva to display his beautiful form. Shiva portrayed his beautiful form. His body shone like a thousand suns and a crown glittered on his head. Maneka was ashamed of her absurdity. She did not further create obstacles in her daughter's marriage. Parvati got married with Lord Shiva and thereafter dwell happily with her husband in Kailash.

Garuda Purana

Garuda Purana consists of many meaningful stories, including the one given below: —

Santaptaka and the Ghosts

In the olden times, there lived a Brahman named Santaptaka, who had renounced the world. He lived in the forests and performed meditation. One day while traversing in the woods of the forests, he came up on a Banyan tree, where five ghosts were eating a dead body.

The ghosts were similar to skeletons, but they did not have any noses. The ghosts were eating the dead body with their teeth and nails. As soon as they saw Santaptaka, they grabbed him tightly. Each one said that he should eat him first.

Santaptaka was frightened He began to pray to Lord Vishnu to save him form the clutches of those troublesome ghosts.

Vishnu heard his prayers. He called upon the King of Yakshas named Manibhadra and directed him to adopt the form of a ghost and fight with other ghosts for the Brahman's body.

Manibhadra obeyed his lord's orders. He became a ghost and fought with other ghosts for the Brahman's body. After the fight was over, the ghosts again returned back to eat the Brahman, but with the grace of Vishnu, they remembered their past lives.

They fell at the feet of Brahman and repented for their misdeeds. Santaptaka forgave them. But he asked them how did they become ghosts. One of the ghosts named Paryushita became ghost when he gave tainted food to a Brahman.

Another ghost named Suchimukha had to suffer the consequences of stealing away the belongings of a woman. Besides this, did not allow her five-year-old son to drink water from the pot. The little boy died out of thirst and fright. The woman committed suicide after the death of her son. Suchimukha became a ghost. His mouth became as small as a needle, so that he could not eat and chew everything comfortably.

Shighragha became a ghost after killing his friend. He and his friend had gone to a distant country to trade. His friend made huge profits but he lost all his capital. His friend was sleeping in his lap when he flung him into the river and killed him. He accumulated his wealth and fled away. After that he gave false report to his wife that her husband has been killed by the bandits.

The grief stricken wife committed suicide by immolating herself in fire.

Rodhaka's story was that he used to be close to a king. The king liked him and thus gave him a hundred villages to rule upon. Rodhaka had a brother, but Rodhaka did not share his property with his brother. His brother lived in poverty. His parents tried to help his brother secretly, but somehow Rodhaka came to know about it. He imprisoned his parents. His parents took poison in the prison and died. The young brother begged for a living, but he too died.

This sin made Rodhaka a ghost. Now he wandered in the forests and lived the miserable life of a ghost. Lekhaka was a Brahman who lived in the City of Avanti. He was employed by the king as the priest. While working in the temple as the priest, Lekhaka was tempted to steal away the jewels and golden ornaments around the images of the gods and goddesses. He then killed the king and fled away with the precious jewels and ornaments. Due to this sin, he became the ghost who wandered into the forests in a form of a skeleton.

The ghosts asked Santaptaka to forgive them for their misdeeds. Their repentance for their misdeeds turned their misfortune into a fortune.

Lord Vishnu descended from his abode and took all of them with Santaptaka to his heavenly abode.

Garuda Purana forbids us to sin. A Sinner becomes a wandering soul and has to languish in the hell.

There are around eighty-four lakhs of hells mentioned in Purana.

There is a hell called Nikrintana in which a Sinner is tied to stakes and their bodies are sliced with sharp chakras. The slicing begins with the feet then moves up the body to the head and then again begins with the feet. The sliced parts join up again.

After the punishments in the hell are over, the Sinner is bound to take birth again. The punishments are very severe for the Sinner; therefore one must fear god and never harm other creatures, who are the children of Almighty God.

Padma Purana

Padma Purana is a sacred text of Hindus. Reading of this text can grant the benefit of numerous good deeds.

All the religious scriptures, including Padma Purana, emphasise on the virtues of forgiveness, tolerance, penance and self-control.

The laws of nature forbid the man to become violent towards innocent people. The woman must obey her husband, if he is respectful towards her and the husband must not compel his wife to do things, which are not of her choice. It is wrong to be cruel to innocent women. There are severe punishments for those men, who are cruel towards their simple-minded wives. "Women" must be respected by the men of the world, and they should protect them from the shrewd elements that exploit, misguide and torture them for vested interests. A story is given below regarding the pathetic condition of the women.

In the olden times, there lived a woman called "Hemaprabha". She was very unhappy with her husband. He used to take a lot of work from her, but never gave any value to her work. He used to insult her and compel her to do everything according to his will; he would beat her up. She was very unhappy with the way her husband behaved with her. She could now no more tolerate any more insults.

One day out of anger, she retired into the bedroom and kept Ekadashi Vrata (fasting of god). She died in night. After her death she was taken to the abode of Lord Vishnu, as she had fasted on the auspicious day (Ekadashi tithi). The man is bound to suffer the outcome of evil actions, if he doesn't repent for his deeds.

Bathing in sacred rivers like Ganga and Reva are highly recommended for the forgiveness of one's sins.

A story of Vikundala portrays the significance of bathing in these auspicious rivers. In the ancient times, there used to live a person named "Hemakundala", who was devoted to gods and demigods. His main occupation was animal husbandry and trade; therefore, he accumulated abundant wealth in these pursuits. His total wealth amounted to eight crores of gold coins.

After becoming old, Hemakundala spent one-sixth of his wealth on virtuous acts like building temples, digging ponds, planting trees and distributing alms to poor people. After that, he divided his wealth between his two sons called "Shrikundala" and "Vikundala" and thereafter went to the forest to meditate.

His sons were not sensible. They were sluggish and senseless. They wasted away their father's hard earned money on luxuries. When they became poor, all the false friends showed their true colours. They deserted them. The two brothers went to the forests and became hunters. While they were in forest, Shrikundala got killed by a tiger and Vikundala was bitten by a poisonous snake.

Both of them died at the same time. After their death, both of them were brought together to Lord Yama.

Yama ordered his messengers to take Shrikundala to the severest of hells and Vikundala to heavens.

Vikundala was perplexed. He asked Lord Yama, why he should go to heaven, when he has performed the same evil acts as his brother.

Lord Yama said that though he had performed the same evil acts of his brother, but since he has taken a bath in a spiritual river, his all sins have been forgiven, whereas his brother never cleaned his sins by taking the bath in the spiritual river. But Vikundala somehow did not agree. He wanted to save his brother from going to the hell.

Thereafter the messenger suggested that the only way to save his brother was to transfer his good deeds in the account of his brother. He further added that eight lives ago, he was a Brahman. He had welcomed the sages in his home and also gave them alms. This virtuous deed could be transferred into the account of his brother Shrikundala, if he was ready for the same.

Vikundala readily agreed to transfer this virtuous deed into the account of his brother. Shrikundala was therefore freed from the punishments of hell, and was sent to the heaven along with his brother.

From this story we come to a conclusion that doing virtuous deeds could reduce the burden of our sins.

Skanda Purana

A story in Skanda Purana emphasises on the truth that gods and demigods created by Almighty God, are not perfect. They are prone to errors like human beings. What makes them superior to human beings is their spiritual powers, which they have acquired through the practice of meditation. God has created Lord Brahma as Creator, Lord Vishnu as Operator and Lord Shiva as Destroyer. These Gods may be superior to all other demigods in respect to spiritual powers, but still they lack perfection. The story given below throws light on this truth.

One day the Sage Narad went to Mount Gandhamadana to meet Shiva. There he found Shiva and Parvati happy in each other's company.

Narad told them to play a game of dice to spend time. Both of them agreed to do so.

Shiva won the game through trickery. He began to tease Parvati. This made Parvati angry. She challenged Shiva for another game. This time it was Parvati who won. Now it was the turn of Parvati to tease Shiva. "I have defeated you Shiva" she teased him. Shiva did not agree, "Don't say like that, my dear. In all the three worlds, there is nobody who can defeat me. I am most powerful." "That maybe true", said Parvati. You may not be conquered by any creature from the three worlds, but I have succeeded in defeating you. Shiva's temper rose. Both of them started quarrelling. Narad took the side of Shiva. He told Parvati to keep quiet, as Shiva was invincible.

She had not defeated Shiva but Shiva had lost the game, willingly. Parvati told him to remain quiet and not to blow up Shiva's importance out of proportion, as she believed that it was she who established him in the universe. Shiva's attendant Bhringi tried to restrain Parvati from being proud, but to no avail. She considered herself superior to Shiva. Shiva went to the forest to escape from the fury of Parvati.

Parvati thought of playing a prank. She transformed herself into a beautiful woman and appeared before Lord Shiva.

Shiva was already angry with Parvati. He thought that Parvati did not love him. He had a misunderstanding about Parvati's feelings for him. In fact, Parvati loved him more than anyone else in the world, but she wanted to eliminate his inflated "Ego". She didn't want that her husband should be proud of his powers, thus, she had told him to accept his defeat in the game from her.

Lord Shiva was captivated with the beautiful damsel's alluring gestures and innocence.

He asked her to marry him. The damsel told him to meet Mount Himalaya, who was her father. Shiva went to meet him. Mount Himalaya told him that he was already his son-in-law, then what for he has come for the marriage proposal. Shiva was embarrassed by the turn of events. He went off to Mount Gandhamadana and began to meditate over there. His wife Parvati came along with the inhabitants of Kailash and chanted hymns in his praise. Shiva returned back and everyone welcomed him with flowers and beating of drums. Shiva was reunited with his beloved wife, Parvati.

From this story we draw a lesson that a husband and wife must not compete with one-another, else, it leads to conflicts, quarrels and fights. One should not be so proud of oneself that others feel let down. Competition should be healthy because unhealthy competition leads to separation of two souls deeply in love.

Brahmavaivarta Purana

The Brahma Vaivarta Purana consists of the sacred texts that portray the creation of gods and men, the nature of gods and goddesses, heavens and hells and cures of different ailments, birth of Lord Ganesh, Krishna's birth and deeds. Here we shall give a few most important texts in the Purana. The creation of the world is discussed in a wonderful manner in holy book Brahma Vaivarta Purana.

At the time of destruction, all the three worlds are destroyed, but the spiritual regions above these three worlds are not destroyed. The three worlds are Earth, Heaven and the region between Earth and Heaven. Above the three worlds are spiritual regions known as Vaikunthaloka, Shivaloka and Goloka. These spiritual regions are not destroyed.

In the beginning, the world was empty and void. There was nothing in the world. Almighty God created the gods, goddesses to help him in the creation of the world. Thereafter the process of creation took place. It is mentioned in this holy scripture that in the beginning of the creation, nobody is a Sinner; therefore it is called "Satyuga". Slowly and gradually, people become corrupt and violent. The negativity of their sins causes natural disasters. The earthquakes, volcanoes and floods destroy the lives of the Sinners. The families break up due to conflicts. Rivers and ponds dry up. Cows stop giving milk. Everything appears in chaos. The negativity of sins causes the human beings to suffer punishments given by the nature.

One of the worst of all sins committed by the human beings is "PRIDE". A proud person always tries to put others down to show his own superiority over them. A proud person doesn't respect others. He demands respect from others but he doesn't himself give any regard to others. Such proud persons are detested by the entire society. Even God condemns them. Other than human beings, the demigods (demi=half god=god) also become proud. Almighty God creates the demigods for the creation, operation and destruction of the universe.

Every proud person is humbled down by the laws of nature.

Here is a story extracted from Brahma Vaivarta Purana that portrays how the laws of nature humble down the proud Lord Shiva.

Since Lord Shiva had acquired many spiritual powers through the practice of meditation on god, he became proud of his powers. He began to grant boons, without thinking of its consequences. A demon called Vrika pleaded before Shiva that Lord Shiva should grant him one boon that whenever he placed his hand on anyone's head, that person should turn to ashes.

Shiva granted him that boon but out of pride. Vrika was such a devil, that he wanted to try out that boon on his benefactor, Shiva himself. Shiva ran here and there to save himself from the clutches of evil demon, but he followed him everywhere. Eventually Shiva took refuge with Vishnu.

Vishnu asked Vrika "How did you come to believe this liar Shiva? Shiva has not granted you any boon. If you don't believe my word, then keep your hands on your head and find out yourself."

Vrika agreed. The moment he kept his hands on his head, he was burnt to ashes. Shiva sang glories of Lord Vishnu for giving him protection from the demon.

Therefore it is clear from this story, that one must not do any irrational act out of pride, else, it causes troubles to the life of a haughty person, who misuses his powers.

Agni Purana

Agni Purana consists of fewer stories but more philosophies. There are varied of subjects like economics, rituals, literature etc. discussed in Agni Purana.

In one of the texts, it is mentioned how to please gods and demigods with the utterance of prayers and mantras (incantation). Cleanliness of mind and body is given special importance in this sacred text.

The dirt of jealousy, pride and anger should be washed away with the water of prayers and meditation to god.

God is further pleased with virtuous acts to such as donation of alms to the needy, building of temples, building of idols of spiritual entities, besides this, visits to pilgrimages also pleases god. Some of the best places of pilgrimages are: —

1. Pushkara
2. Kurukshetra
3. Prayaga
4. Varanasi, and
5. Gaya

The man should be protective and responsible towards his wife. He should give her a little freedom to do things in her own way. He should not make her his slave, nor should he suppress her beyond limits. To disrespect one's wife is a great sin. A person who doesn't give value to his wife's work, lands up straight away to hell. A woman must be faithful to her husband and adjust with his family members. She must give love and respect to her husband and his family members and consider every other man as her brother, except her husband.

The leader of the country or the King must not spend the country's money on his own comforts and luxuries. The country's wealth must be spent for the removal of poverty and unemployment. Else, the laws of nature give severest punishments to the selfish kings and leaders.

After the death, the human beings acquire new bodies that are similar to the physical bodies that they have given up. Thereafter they are taken away by the Lord of Justice in his abode. There, his virtuous acts and deeds are judged. If the meritorious acts measure more than the evil deeds, then he is sent to heaven, else he is sent to hell. After that, he again takes birth.

A person should practice "Yoga" to lead a healthier life.

Yoga means union of the soul with super soul.

A person should do deep breathing exercise in fresh air in the morning hours. Some yogic exercises like Padmasan are extremely beneficial for health. In this, left palm is kept on right leg and right palm is kept on left leg. The arms rest on the folded thighs.

This is also called Lotus position. It is extremely beneficial for health if done for twenty minutes daily. Agni Purana is one of the most sacred books of Hindus. Hearing of its texts eliminates the negativities of sins and brings good health, wealth and prosperity in the house. If one hears a recital of the Agni Purana, the sins committed over the duration of the day are forgiven. If one reads a text of Agni Purana daily, the thieves, dacoits and ghosts remain at bay. Reading of this wonderful scripture brings good fortune in one's life.

Glimpse of Vedas

The Vedas are sacred texts of Hindus. The word "Veda" means knowledge. There are four Vedas–Rig Veda, Yajur Veda, Sama Veda and Atharva Veda. The Vedas consist of prayers to Almighty God and all the prominent gods and goddesses of the Universe.

Some of the prayers are given below: —

Kena Surta (from what?)

Who created the universe that we see? From what was the universe made? Where did I come from? Where will I go? Who created the men? Who created the flesh and the handsome figures?

Who is the one who specially preserved the Earth? The God is the one who placed Heaven above Earth. The God is the one who placed vast atmosphere above Earth.

The one who successfully meditates, controls his head and heart. He raises his life force to the centre of his head and even above his head.

The God is spread everywhere. It is in every direction. The city where he lives is full of energy. The city removes all miseries.

In one of the prayers, Lord Agni is glorified, so that he could shower blessings to his devotees, according to the spiritual powers granted to him by Almighty God.

Prayer to Lord Agni (Fire)

O Omniscient Agni! You are acquainted with all objects. Destroy all our enemies. Protect us from enemies who have yet not emerged. Do not forsake us, but grant us boons with a benevolent heart.

O Agni! You are the shining one. Your tongues are as sharp as the Vajra. You are famous as the destroyer of the demons. Destroy the demons that are here during the day and destroy the ones who are here at time of dawn.

Prayer to God

May the supreme God grant everyone the wisdom to perform righteous deeds and protect righteousness. May the Supreme God purify us and purify our learning. May our speech become sweet and may we tread superior paths.

We meditate on the energy of the Supreme Godhead. It is this energy that inspires our intelligence.

O Supreme Godhead! You are the creator. Keep all-evil away from us and keep us close to all that is good.

In one text of Yajur Veda, it is mentioned that different people should be employed for the completion of different work.

Fishermen should be employed to take care of lakes and ponds. People should be employed to take care of small ponds.

The water in these ponds must be regularly be cleaned. Those who can swim well must be employed near rivers and ponds to prevent others from drowning. Employ musicians to obtain a good voice. Employ hunters to live in caves.

Employ jewellers who work with gold. Employ tradesmen and shopkeepers to measure weights. Be skilled, to attain superiority. If one is lazy, downfall is certain. Be humble to attain superiority. To deal with Sun, employ one whose eyes are Green; to deal with the Stars, employ one whose eyes are Orange. To deal with the Moon, employ one whose eyes are White.

The Supreme God has abundance of riches and is the lord of everyone. He brings welfare to bipeds and quadrupeds.

I pray to the one who removes all evil. I pray to the one who increases purity. I pray to the one whose energy radiates out. The Supreme God who purifies everything will bring all of us welfare.

One of the prayers called "Manasa" is quite soulful. It refers to the spirit of a person who is about to die. It is prayed before God to revive the person from death, and grant him more years on the earth.

Manasa (Spirit)

Your spirit has gone far away,

Yama is the son of Vivasvana.

Your spirit has gone to Yama.

May your spirit come back,

You have been born that,

You may live in this world.

Your spirit has gone far away. It has gone near Heaven and the Earth. May your spirit return. You have been born, so that you may live in this world.

Your spirit has gone far away. It has reached the Earth, which is heated from the four directions (refers to "desert"). May your spirit return, you have been born, so that you may live on this Earth.

Your spirit has gone far away. It has reached the water of the ocean. May your spirit return. You have been born, so that you may live in this world.

Your spirit has gone far away. It has reached the rays that radiate out in the four directions. May your spirit return. You have been born, so that you may live in this world.

Your spirit has gone far away. It has reached the water, the trees and herbs. May your spirit return. You have been born, so that you may live in this world.

Your spirit has gone far away. It has reached the past and the future. May your spirit return. You have been born, so that you may live in this world.

In Atharva Veda, the definition of the soul is given in a most wonderful way. This text throws light on the proper definition of human soul; what is human soul and how could it be purified.

The Human Soul

There are four ways to purify the human soul. The first is to concentrate one's mind through meditation so that one realises the origin of all speech. The second is to be always truthful. The third is to follow the path of learning, and the fourth is to keep chanting name of Parmatman (God). The Supreme Soul is sweet and immortal. The soul must elevate itself through meditation, so that it can unite with supreme soul.

The World Beyond

This is not the only world created by omnipotent god; there are many worlds beyond this world.

All the worlds are generated, operated and destroyed by the supreme energy of god. Almighty God has created innumerable living beings, ghosts, evil spirits, gods and goddesses. There are no limits of his creation. God is everlasting soothing powerful light of energy that can fulfil all prayers and create, operate and destroy the entire world within a fraction of a second.

Beyond this world, there are many worlds; some worlds are in the process of creation, and others are already established by the power of Supreme Energy of God.

There is a world of demigods, enveloped with a beautiful environment. The lush green trees, blooming flowers, golden palaces and elegant ponds attribute beauty in the heavens.

There is a world of evil spirits, ghosts and giants. The evil spirits are very troublesome. They make the person's life a living hell. Sometimes they kill innocent people. Only spiritually inclined people are able to protect themselves from their clutches, other people have to suffer.

Evil spirit is no illusion or delusion. It is a reality. It is mentioned in all religious scriptures, including Vedas, that the ghosts and evil spirits do have a world of their own. Sometimes they haunt in lonely forests and solitude bungalows. I myself have seen evil spirits.

I remember just a few years back, after the death of my sister, I saw her spirit haunting in our rented house. We were staying in a 3-room set in Pandav Nagar, when my sister died. She committed suicide due to depression. In fact, we were undergoing bad circumstances at that time. My father was working in a company. He had made a report against a few corrupt officers, who had misappropriated the accounts of the company. My father was serving as the Chief Internal Auditor when he made the report against corrupt officers. The corrupt officers dismissed him from the job after framing false charges against him. After that, we had to suffer a lot. After leading a luxurious life of aeroplanes, bungalows, servants, we were left penniless. I was the only bread earner of the family. Our relatives gave us only a little help. They refused to help us more. My sister died after consuming poison. She wrote a letter stating that no harm should be done to us, as we were innocent and she was taking that step with her own will. We all were deeply grieved at her death.

After her death, I saw her spirit haunting at our rented house. Sometimes, I would see her looking at the mirror, sometime she would become a cat and other times she would sing sad songs. One day, I saw something written on the walls with red colour. It was my pet name, "Meenu, I have not got salvation". I was shocked. How did my sister not get salvation? She was very devoted to God and had got a small medal from Guiness Book of World Records for writing "God" for the greatest number of times. Then I thought maybe that my sister had not taken God's name before death. It is very essential to take God's name with utmost devotion to God, while dieing, else one lands up into miseries. When one dies, one should be desireless and should not have any more wishes except to meet God and dwell in his abode with him. My sister, Omneeta didn't do so. Perhaps she didn't take God's name before death.

After seeing my sister in such a miserable state, I became very depressed. I remember how I used to love my sister when she was alive. I used to bring delicious food for her from the market, take care of her, when she was in the hospital, tolerate her when she abused me or beat me, due to madness of mind, I tolerated her and despite of that I loved her and did everything to make her happy. Now that she was suffering in hell, I thought of granting her salvation through prayers. One day I saw my dead sister sitting before me and crying while keeping her hands on her face. I got scared. Thereafter saw her sitting in front of me, and gazing at me continuously with her black eyes. She was in fact trying to hypnotise me. After looking at her, I found that I am getting hypnotised through the magnetic power of her eyes. Since I already knew about hypnotism, therefore, I refused to be hypnotised. I immediately stopped gazing at her eyes, through which she was hypnotising me. In fact, her soul intention was to kill me. Thereafter she tried to kill me at four o'clock in the morning but every time I escaped death. I was surprised I had always wanted the welfare of my sister, but she had an intention to kill me. One day I saw my sister in a form of beautiful damsel and the other day I saw her in a dangerous form. Now, I wished to grant salvation to my sister, I knew the only way to do that was to pray to Almighty God. I was very attached to my sister in spite of her misbehaviour towards me. Though I don't allow anybody else to misbehave with me and give a good scolding to people who are cruel towards me but I loved my sister and I tolerated her out of kindness and love.

After watching her in such a pathetic condition, I thought of meditating on God to seek her salvation. I started meditating on God. After 36 hours of deep meditation, she finally got freedom. Before going she uttered "Thank you, Meenu, for granting me salvation". After thanking me she went away to dwell with God.

Therefore, we must accept the truth, as mentioned in all religious scriptures and experienced by people like me. There is a world of spirits too, beyond this world. Some of us consider it a superstition, but it is a truth. We don't give knowledge to our children about such things, considering they would become fearful, but we are wrong. We must impart the knowledge about that truth to them, so that their fears should eliminate if they happen to see them by chance. These things can't harm us if we take God's name.

Here are some methods, through which we can save ourselves from such kind of things: —

(1) Firstly, understand that God is in the form of soothing blissful light, just like the sun, but its not hot like sun. It's cool light of energy. Our soul is also a small part of God's light. God has expanded his energy and created all the worlds including living beings. Our soul is a tiny form of God's expanded energy. God's energy is positive. Our sins form negative energy of black colour in our Aura. It is due to the black energy of our sins, that we suffer diseases and tribulations in life. When we pray to God, we call upon his white coloured energy. The white coloured energy of God eliminates the black coloured energy of our sins.

    The energy of God can be called through many ways. We can call it through spiritual hymns, Reiki and by writing those words, which are dear to him. One of the prayers to eliminate the negativity of evil spirits is given below: —

    OM NAMO KALI KAPALI DAHI DANI SVAHA

    This prayer has to be uttered on oil. Utter this prayer for 1100 times on the oil, thereafter, massage that oil on the body. This method creates spiritual vibrations that save from spirits.

(2) Close your eyes, concentrate in the midst of two eyebrows and recite "OM" everyday.

(3) Read Sundarkand (religious scriptures based on Lord Hanuman).

(4) Go through Gayatri Mantra. Chant 108 Mantras in morning and evening.

(5) Pray to God at 4 am every day for at least twenty days. It shall also give you relief.

(6) The best thing is to read the religious scriptures of your choice daily in the evening. That shall give you protection from the evil spirits.

There is not only the world of evil spirits, but there are several worlds beyond that.

Our maidservant tells us that one day while digging a well, she saw a small man. He died after that. The man was very small. He had beard and moustache. One man told us, that he died twice. After death, he saw God's administrator of justice, Yama, who took him to hell. Since the man had more years of life on the earth, he was sent back. Another man, of his name was sent to hell.

The man also saw small men living in water, beautiful fairies and other damsels. Another man I knew is also like a brother to me and has family relations with us.

He told me that after death, he saw Goddess Lakshmi. She showered blessings upon him and told him that he shall not be in lack of money. After that he was sent back to life.

I read in a magazine, the experiences of people who came back to life after death. A lady mentioned that she committed suicide when her lover betrayed her in love. He got married to someone else. She committed suicide. After her death, she found herself in the world of ghosts. The ghosts began to pierce her body into pieces With a sad mind, she began to pray to God to release her from this miserable condition. After repeated prayers to God, she came back to life. She found herself in the operation theatre. This portrays that a person who commits suicide without meditating on God, lands up in hell. But if a person commits suicide after meditating on God or God's messengers, he goes up to the spiritual realms.

My father's sister's husband, Doctor Sinha uncle was very devoted to "Sai Baba". Sai Baba is one of the most respected spiritual entities, who became one with God, by chanting his names. Dr. Sinha was very devoted to Sai Baba. He was not happy with life. He had left his first wife, who was otherwise very beautiful and talented. She was a classical dancer. He had some conflicts with her and he left her. After leaving her, he got married to my aunt. He was not happy with my aunt, therefore, he ended his life, but before his death, he prayed to

Sai Baba to call him in his abode after death. After his cremation, I got to see his Aatmaraam. Aatmaraam is a part of skull, in the middle of two eyebrows, where the soul resides. In that, I saw the form of Sai Baba. That portrays that he mingled with Sai Baba after death, though he committed suicide, yet, God forgave all his sins, as he uttered prayers to him in faith.

My maternal grandfather was a god-fearing person. He remained hale and hearty throughout his life, as he used to get up in early hours of the morning and pray to God daily. He died a very peaceful death. He didn't have to face much sufferings and tribulations in his life. He didn't suffer from chronic diseases. He didn't have to lie down on the bed for many years. He had intution about his death. He told his son-in-law that it was his time to leave the world, therefore, he should bid him goodbye. After saluting his son-in-law, he went to the hospital. He was suffering from fever. He chanted holy names of God, meditated on God and died peacefully. My maternal grandfather died a peaceful death but paternal grandfather died a miserable death. He never used to take God's name. Before his death, he had to suffer a lot. He became unconscious all of a sudden.

My father admitted him into a hospital. He remained unconscious for several days. Before his death, he called up my grandmother and told her that he saw someone coming. He told the unknown person to go away, but he was not leaving him. He was in fact God's administrator of justice, Lord Yama, who had come to take his soul away. My grandfather died in the hospital. I saw him dying. His breathing became heavy before his death. After that he died. I loved both of my grandfathers. But there was a world of difference between their nature and temperaments. My maternal grandfather was a god-fearing person, whereas my paternal grandfather never believed in God. Both of them died different kinds of death. From these experiences, it is clear that there are many worlds beyond this world, and if we want to lead a blissful life in this world and the worlds beyond, we must chant holy names of

God in the early hours of morning. Simply utter the most simple prayer "God, grant me health, wealth, success and salvation after death". This simple prayer, if done with closed eyes, concentrating in the middle of the eyebrows, will do wonders in your life and grant you and your beloved ones abundant happiness.

How Demigods are not God?

Demigods may have spiritual powers to a certain extent, but they are not God. Now the question arises, why they are not? They are not God, because, they are not all powerful like God, they have restricted spiritual powers. Secondly, they are not perfect like God, they are prone to commit errors, thirdly they have to pray or meditate on God to acquire spiritual powers, whereas God doesn't have to meditate to acquire those powers, he is all powerful, blissful, soothing light of energy, who can create, operate and destroy the entire world within a fraction of a second.

The demigods are created by God to run the worlds, efficiently. They are prone to errors. Now, let's go through their stories to find out what blunders did various demigods commit in their lives. Brahma developed physical relations with Goddess Saraswati, who was his own daughter. Shiva got proud of his spiritual powers and started giving boons to devils, without thinking about the consequences; he also slashed of the head of his son "Ganesh" out of pride. Goddess Saraswati was jealous of Ganga. One day she fought with her and tried to grasp by her hair. Demigod Indra was so arrogant about his spiritual powers, that he insulted Goddess Nature, by ignoring her. Goddess Nature then cursed him that he shall be cursed by his own guru.

From these examples it is clear that Gods and Demigods (half-gods) are not perfect as Almighty God. They are not pure as God. They are not powerful as God. They may have spiritual powers, but their spiritual powers are limited, whereas

God has limitless spiritual powers. They are prone to follies like humans whereas God is blameless. He doesn't commit any errors. Therefore it is clearthat Demigods are NOT "GOD"

How to Judge A True Saint

It is very difficult to find out a true saint these days. Most of the people pretend to be a saint in order to accumulate money from others, but they are not truly devoted to God. Though its a complicated task to judge a true saint, yet, we can judge them to some extent by applying the following methods: —

(1) Observe, whether there is a glow in his face. A spiritually inclined person rarely gets sick. His face is radiant and glowing, as his aura becomes high with the chanting of holy names of God, but not every person who is of glowing health is a saint, but a saint is certainly of glowing health. If you observe the pictures of the ancient sages, you will find them in glowing health.

(2) A true saint may want money to fulfil his needs, but he is not greedy for money. He doesn't want more wealth than what is required for his necessities. A greedy man is not a true saint. He is befooling people.

(3) A true saint cares for poor people. He doesn't disrespect poor people. If poor people are foolish, and they annoy him by limitless demands, then he corrects them, but he doesn't admonish poor people who are sensible. He only chides troublesome people, but not sensible people.

(4) A true saint opens up free orphanages, old-age homes, and temples for poor people. He doesn't take any money from poor people, but accepts donations from wealthy people. If a true saint doesn't have enough money to establish free homes for poor people, then, he makes

them tread on the right path through virtuous deeds and truthful speech.

(5) A true saint doesn't pretend to be kind. He is naturally kind. He doesn't open up institutions to earn name and fame. His sole intention is to do good to others without any obligations. These are the traits of a true saint. A true saint forgets, forgivess and corrects others.

Evil and Good Omen—
How far are they true?

There are some educated and illiterate people in the world, who live in the darkness of ignorance and believe in superstitions. Some of them believe that if a cat crosses the path, while a person is on his way to some work, then, he shall face obstacles in his work. One sparrow is believed to bring ill luck and two sparrows are believed to bring good fortune. People who believe in such kind of superstitions, are groping in the darkness of ignorance.

In truth, you are the creator of your destiny. Your past deeds make your destiny. If your past deeds are good, you are sure to be rewarded in future. The rewards may come in the form of good job, wealth, success in work etc., and if your deeds are evil, then you are sure to suffer punishments in the form of imprisonment, defame etc.

Sometimes even good people also have to suffer, but their case is different. They have to undergo tests given by God, as Almighty God wants to test them, how good they are. If they undergo the test in the form of sufferings and tribulations given by God, then they are given abundant honour and rewards in his abode. Good people are put into a test, while bad people suffer consequences of their misdeeds.

There is no good and evil omen as such. These things are false. Just wonder what would happen to a man who believes in such false things. Take an example of a superstitious fellow called Mr. X. He is going for an interview. A black cat crosses his way. Since he believes in such kind of superstitions, he goes back to his home thinking that he would not be selected for the interview. But his father is a knowledgeful person. He doesn't believe in such kind of superstitions. He tells him to attend the interview, whatever the result might be.

Mr. X attends the interview and is selected for the job. Now he repents for believing in such kind of superstitions.

This is realistic fiction. This happens with people in real life. They create obstacles in their life by believing in such things. Now, it is said that one sparrow brings ill luck. If a person believes in this omen, then he is certain to remain a failure in his life. Wherever he shall see one sparrow, he shall believe that he is going to be in trouble that day. He shall keep on worrying about that trouble whole day and avoid all his work in his depressed state of mind. He may not be in any trouble otherwise, but he shall certainly create trouble by believing in such kind of things. Therefore, if you want to make a success of your life then don't believe in such kind of omens, but believe in God, who is your best friend. He shall save you from all troubles and tribulations. Believe me, God has fulfilled all of my prayers and saved me from all troubles, whenever I have called him up with faith. Therefore, don't make your life miserable by groping in the darkness of ignorance, lit up the torch of knowledge and utter a prayer to God everyday to grant you success, health, wealth and happiness.

How to Eliminate the Negativity of Your House?

Some houses send negative vibrations in the environment. There are many factors responsible for the negativity of the house. If the house is located in negative surroundings, it attains negativity, if a person dies young in the house, and his cremation rites are not done properly, then too the house attains negativity. To eliminate the negativity of the house, you may apply any one or two of the given methods: —

(1) Utter a prayer to Lord Ganesh everyday. One of the best prayers is given below: —

O Destroyer of multitudes of obstacles!
O Askew Trunked!
O Dweller in thy own names like Ganesh and others.
O Four-Armed!
O Lord of Poets!
O Destroyer of Demons–so saying,
O Human being get rid of your fright.

Utter this prayer on a glass of water, and sprinkle that nectar on each room of your house everyday.

(2) Make a chart of the word "OM" (ॐ) and cling it in anyone room of your house.

(3) Utter this prayer on a glass of water with closed eyes and sprinkle it in every room.O Lord! O Shambho! O God! I neither know anything about penance or ritual worship. O

Shambho! I ever regard you only! Please redeem me from the afflictions of sorrow and protect me by your grace!(4) Lit up a candle before the idol of your favourite God and pray to him every day.

(5)Read any text from the religious scripture of your choice, everyday.

These methods are simple but extremely effective. They shall bring abundant joy and prosperity in your life.

Problems and Solutions of Life

Every one of us has one or the other problem in life, but we don't have any solution for it. What should we do when we are surrounded with problems of life? Here is some sound advice! This lesson shall enhance your sensibility in finding out many solutions of life. You can take your own decisions after that.

Problem I

Mr. Thomas is in a confused state of mind. His mother and wife had a terrible fight. His mother tells his wife to sit at home and do the household work, whereas his wife wants to work outside and keep a part-time maid for household tasks. His mother got annoyed with his wife. She beat her and threatened to kill her. His wife started weeping. Mr. Thomas doesn't know what to do.

Solution: In this example, Mr. Thomas's mother is wrong. She is cruel towards her daughter-in-law. She doesn't give her to least freedom, and wants her to do everything according to her will. Mr. Thomas must stop his mother from hurting his wife. He should also allow his wife to do a respectable job outside the premises of his house, provided she keeps her character strong, and remains faithful to him.

Problem 2

Mr. Garg is fed up of his wife. His wife goes to the nightclubs and ignores her family. Daily, she goes outside to enjoy herself in nightclubs, while her babies feel ignored. What should Garg do?

Solution: Mr. Garg should ask his wife the reason, why she doesn't stay at home to take care of her children? If she says that she enjoys outside, then he should tell her that this way, her life would be rather miserable, as she would not be able to get the love of her children and husband. Thereafter Garg should tell his wife that she should either take care of her family or take the divorce. In case, she corrects herself, well and fine, otherwise, he should take divorce and keep a decent governess to take care of the children. In case, he gets an issueless widow woman, who aggress to take care of his children, as her own without having her own children, he may marry her.

Problem 3

Mrs. Gita is going to attend an important meeting. On the way she finds two women fighting with each other. Matters are getting exaggerated. As a good citizen, what should Mrs. Gita do?

Solution: The best way to solve the quarrel is to SEPARATE the two persons, or groups who are fighting with each other. Take them away from one another and don't allow them to come near one another till they are peaceful, and agree to compromise with each other.

Problem 4

You are a good-hearted person. You want to give financial and moral support to people in distress, but people start taking benefit of your kindness. They keep of your kindness. They keep on demanding things from you out of greed. After you fulfil one demand, they demand another things from you and so on. Their demands never end. People also become jealous, when they see you giving things to others. They are tempted to the things that you give to others and want things for themselves.

Solution: These kind of people are shrewd, selfish and greedy. They don't have compassion for others. You must bluntly tell them to keep themselves at distance attributing that since it's your hard earned money, therefore you have every right to use it in your own way. Moreover, you are giving help to the needy people, not the greedy people. People should only come to you in dire need and they must not compete with others. Rather, they should help the poor people to stand on their feet. God gives dire punishments to shrewd people, who trouble good-hearted people and talk ill of them behind their backs.

Problem 5

You have kept a servant. He is greedy. He behaves nicely with you, but inwardly, wants to steal away your wealth and run away. How shall you test him?

Solution: To judge whether your servant is faithful to you or not, throw away a hundred rupee not on the ground. If the servant keeps it with himself, he is a thief, and if he gives back to you, he is honest towards you. Do this act two or three times, but your servant must not come to know that you are intentionally doing that, else, he shall pretend to be honest by giving that money back to you, though he may be dishonest inside.

Keep your money safe in a cupboard, and keep the key of your cupboard in your purse. Don't allow the servant to enter your house when you are alone, your husband and children should be there with you. Don't allow the servant's acquaintances to enter in your house. Keep them outside. Remember, it's very dangerous to have faith in your servants these days. They can steal away your entire wealth out of greed, and make you bankrupt. It is better to keep maidservants, who are not very strong built like males. You should otherwise be kind towards your servants, and keep on distributing wealth and clothes to them on festivals. Be strict to them only when they are greedy and trouble you with limitless demands.

Problem 6

Mr. Lucky and his wife are greatly displeased with the behaviour of their young son. He is not paying attention to his career but wastes away his parents' money in useless pursuits like wine, gambling, going to the nightclubs etc. What should they do?

Solution: Both of them should develop a friendly approach towards him. They should take him along with them to temples, picnic spots, parks and gardens. They may also take him to watch a good movie together. But this indulgence in luxuries must not cross limits. Take him along with you once a week or twice a month. It's unwise to spend much money on luxuries. Sit with him daily for one hour and talk to him about his plans for future and other sensible topics. Crack sensible jokes with him sometimes. If you shall develop loving and friendly approach towards your children, they would find joy with you and would not indulge in crazy things that ruin their own career and lives.

Problem 7

Baby's daughter-in-law doesn't obey her. She does opposite to what Baby says. Baby remains annoyed with her.

Solution: In fact some mother-in-laws like Baby don't know how to handle their daughter-in-laws. They always keep on watching them do their work. They also keep on criticising them on small things to show their own superiority over them. Their daughter-in-laws become rebellious and obstinate. The best solution to their problem is that they must not always keep on watching their daughter-in-laws do their work, neither should they criticise them before people. They must rather give suggestions and advice, once or twice a month, away from the public eye. They should also appreciate them when they work efficiently. They must take care of them in their sickness, and give them abundant love and respect, so that they should feel honoured in the house. This way they would start obeying them.

Problem 8

Mrs. Elizabeth is a good mother-in-law, but her daughter-in-law is not sensible. She doesn't do any kind of work and leaves every work on her mother-in-law.

Solution: In this example, Mrs. Elizabeth's daughter-in-law is wrong. She doesn't care for her mother-in-law who loves her. Mrs. Elizabeth must ask her the reason about this kind of senseless attitude with her. She should attribute that, she does not only love her son, but her daughter-in-law as well, and she wants the same kind of love and respect from them. How can a person love anyone, who doesn't love him? Love begets love. Mrs. Elizabeth should add that every member of the house must divide their work, according to their stamina and energy. Since older members have less energy, they should be given less work than the younger members, who have more energy.

Mrs. Elizabeth should share the work with her daughter-in-law and chat with her while doing the work. They should wok together, without criticising one another to pull other down. This is one of the best solutions to bring love and harmony in the house.

Problem 9

Mrs. Lovelin's son is very obstinate. He has done his computer post-graduate diploma but is not interested in doing the job. He also doesn't have his food properly.

Solution: She should utter prayer to God at sharp 4 o'clock in the morning, to grant wisdom to her son. Morning prayers are heard very soon by God, and 4 o'clock is auspicious time, therefore her prayers would certainly be heard, if she prays to God with faith. If her son is not interested in doing the job, then, she should open up and institute for him at some authorised colony. There, he can give coaching to the students who want to learn computer and internet. If her son doesn't have his food at home, that means that he may not be getting the dishes of his choice at home. Mrs. Lovelin should join some cooking classes and make delightful dishes of her son's choice.

Problem 10

Mr. David and his wife are not sincere to one another. They seek greener pastures somewhere else, then in each other's company. Mr. David has relationships with many other girls, and his wife has a boy friend. Both of them are unfaithful to their life-partners.

Solution: Most of the couple betray their life partners due to wrong thinking. If a husband talks to a girl like a sister, the wife becomes suspicious and if a wife talks to a man considering him a brother, the husband suspects her relationship with that man. The husband and wife must be true to one another. They must consider other people as brothers and sister and talk to them frankly with a clean heart. They should not suspect one another and should remain faithful to each other.

Problem 11

Mr. Robin is in a very troubled mind-state these days. From the last few days, an evil spirit is giving him nightmares and hypnotising his mind, to bring it under its control. What should he do to save himself from the evil spirit?

Solution: He should plant basil plants in his house. It's positive energy keeps the evil spirits at bay. If the evil spirit is very strong and it doesn't leave the place in spite of that, then he should make 6 charts of letters "OM". In each chart, OM should be written 100 times. Then he should put these charts in the walls of the room, where he sleeps. He should also write the word Om in his finger rings. If the evil spirit is extremely powerful and it doesn't leave the place with these methods, then go through any text of your favourite religious book, everyday, such as "Ramayana", "Gita", or "Sunderkand". Also recite the name of your favourite spiritual entity (such as "Ram") in a glass of water and drink it. You should apply these methods even though you are not troubled by any evil spirit at present, as these methods would protect you from black magicians and evil spirits in future. Remember that the evil spirits hypnotise the minds of the people and make them do things, that bring them defame in the society. They also create obstacles in their way to success.

Problem 12

Mr. Vicky is very worried about his daughter's marriage. His daughter's marriage in scheduled for the next month, but he doesn't have enough money to organise it with pomp and show.

Solution: –There is no such need to organise it in a lavish scale, if one doesn't have enough money. He can do simple marriage in a temple and arrange a decent party afterwards, inviting a limited number of people in the party.

If he doesn't want to do it in this manner, then arrange tents in the park with the stereo system. He may keep a few delightful dishes such as two vegetables made up of Cheese, Buttered Pulse (Makhani Dal), vegetables made up of Gram, Rajma and one sweet dish like Kheer. May add Puris, Naans, and Rice. No need to add more things in the party. The dishes should be less in numbers but delightful. You may get twenty thousand for daughter's marriage from Government. For that you may go to the place from where you get Ration card. They shall give you the information about it. You may also get loans from the bank for the same.

Problem 13

You are living in a rented house. The landlord is very troublesome. He keeps on increasing your rent after every sometime. He also makes big issues out of small and creates furs on trifles. You want to buy a house, but you don't have enough money. What should you do?

Solution: These days you can buy a house without spending much money. You get housing loans from HDFC bank, which you can repay back in installments. Some organisations like DDA, provide housing loans to you without much hassle. You may go to any nearest DDA office and get information about it. Besides this, utter morning prayers to Almighty God asking him to provide you a small but comfortable house to stay in.

Problem 14

You are observing that government employees and clerks are not doing their duty efficiently. If you go to the office to seek Ration card, they don't provide you immediately, if you go for old age pension, they tell you to come again and again, if you go for some complaint, they don't listen to you. What should you do?

Solution: As a citizen of our nation, it's the duty of every one of us to solve this problem that is harming our nation and creating hindrances in its progress and prosperity. The national wealth should be used for the welfare of poor people, not for manufacturing up of spacecrafts, when the nation is enveloped with poverty. As a citizen, you should gather a few people and go along with them to get things done efficiently. You should also write letters, along with your companions, seeking justice from the concerned authorities. Remember your language must be polite and loving, else, people would not listen to you, in spite of the fact that they are wrong.

These solutions are simple and brilliant. Besides this, you must pray to God everyday to grant you success in your efforts in the right direction.

Spiritual Quiz

Here we are giving you a number of quiz papers based on Hindu religious scriptures. This is a different type of quiz divided into many parts. You will have to go through all the papers once and know their answers. After going through once, attend all the questions and find out the percentage. If you get between 90% to 100% questions right, you are excellent, if you fare between 80% to 90% you are very good, if you fare between 70% to 80% you are good and below that you are average. These questions are more than hundred number, therefore find out the percentage through calculation. This quiz shall enhance your knowledge about Hindu scriptures.

Quiz 1

Lord Brahma

Q 1 What was the colour of the egg from which Lord Brahma took birth?

Q 2 What is Lord Brahma better known as–the creator, the operator or the destroyer?

Q 3 The whole universe is divided into five elements–space, water, wind, fire and what next?

Q 4 How many heads does Brahma have?

Q 5 How many arms does Brahma have?

Q 6 What does the name "Vidhata" mean?

Q 7 Who is the husband of Goddess Saraswati?

Q 8 Who is the husband of Goddess Gayatri?

Q 9 Hiranyaksha was a deadly demon. What does his name mean?

Q 10 Hiranyakshapu was Hiranyaksha's brother. In which form did Lord Vishnu kill him?

Q 11 Who is the Goddess of Knowledge?

Q 12 What is the name of the given Mantra (incantation)—

OM BHOOR BHUVA SVA TATSAVITUR VARENYAM
BHARGO DEVASYA DHEEMAHI DHEE YO
YONAH PRACHOODAYATA

Q 13 Who was the father of Bhrigu?

Q 14 Whose face did Lord Vishnu give to Narad, when he asked for a beautiful face to attract the attention of a princess?

Q 15 Who is the father of Narad?

Answers

1. Golden
2. The Creator
3. Earth
4. Five
5. Four
6. The Destiny Maker
7. Brahma
8. Brahma
9. Golden eyes
10. Narasimha (man-lion)
11. Saraswati

12. Gayatri Mantra
13. Brahma
14. Monkey's face
15. Brahma

Quiz 2

Lord Vishnu

Q 1 What does the word "Vishnu" mean?

Q 2 The word "Nara" means water, and "Ayan" refers to "dwelling place"? What does "Narayan" mean?

Q 3 Who is Lord Vishnu's wife?

Q 4 In which hand does Lord Vishnu hold the conch?

Q 5 In which hand does Lord Vishnu hold the Lotus?

Q 6 Lakshmi Narayana temple is a magnificent temple of Lord Vishnu situated at Connaught place. Who built this wonderful temple?

Q 7 Who found Badrinath temple situated in Rishikesh?

Q 8 Where is Vaman temple situated?

Q 9 One of the names devoted to Lord Vishnu is Pootatma: what does that mean?

Q 10 What does the term "Rudrah"mean?

Answers

1. To Pervade
2. One who has water as dwelling place
3. Goddess Lakshmi
4. Right hand
5. Left hand
6. Birlas
7. Adi Shankaracharya

8. Khajuraho
9. The Soul purified
10. One who removes the cause of Sorrow.

Quiz 3

Shiva

Q 1 Who is called the Destroyer of the World?

Q 2 One of the names devoted to Lord Shiva is "Pashupati" What does that mean?

Q 3 Who was Lord Shiva's first wife?

Q 4 Who was Lord Shiva's second wife?

Q 5 Who was Lord Ganpati's mother?

Q 6 Who was Demon Andhak's mother?

Q 7 Whose worship is done on Linga?

Q 8 Who is called Shankar?

Q 9 Which is the favourite ornament of Lord Shankar?

Q 10 Whose worship is done on Mahashivaratri?

Answers

1. Lord Shiva
2. The Master of Animal World
3. Sati
4. Parvati
5. Parvati
6. Parvati
7. Lord Shiva
8. Lord Shiva
9. Rudraksha
10. Lord Shiva's

Quiz 4

Lord Ram

Q 1 Who was the youngest wife of King Dashrath? (a) Kashalaya (b) Kaikeyi (c) Sumitra

Q 2 Ram's birth is celebrated with great pomp and show all over India. What is the auspicious occasion of his birthday called?

Q 3 Who cursed Dashrath, when he killed Shravan Kumar considering him a beast?

Q 4 Who redeemed Ahalya from the curse?

Q 5 Who went to the forests to request Ram's return to Ayodhya? (a) Bharat (b) Shatrughan (c) Lakshman

Q 6 How many years of exile did Kaikeyi give to Ram?

Q 7 What was the name of the sister of Ravana, who gave marriage proposal to Ram?

Q 8 He was Ravan's son. He used black magic and became invisible to pierce arrows in the bodies of the monkeys. Who was he?

Q 9 Which weapon did Ram use to kill Demon Ravana?

Q 10 Which demoness protected Sita when she stayed in Ashok Vatika?

Answers

1. (b) Kaikeyi
2. Ram Navmi
3. Shravan Kumar's father (He cursed that as he was dieing in the unbearable separation of his son, he shall also die in the same way).
4. Lord Ram
5. (a) Bharat
6. Fourteen years

7. Shoorpanakha
8. Meghnath
9. Brahma Weapon
10. Trijata

Quiz 5

Lord Krishna

Q 1 Who was the eighth incarnation of Lord Vishnu?

Q 2 How was Kansa related to Lord Krishna?

Q 3 Which dreaded serpent polluted the River Yamuna during Kansa'a reign?

Q 4 How many children did Devaki give birth to, before Krishna was born?

Q 5 How was Vasudeva related to Krishna?

Q 6 How was Devaki related to Krishna?

Q 7 Who was Krishna's adopted mother?

Q 8 Which demon came to kill Krishna, when he was playing under a bullock cart?

Q 9 He assumed the form of a calf to kill Krishna and Balram when they were playing on the bank of Yamuna. Who was he?

Q 10 Who assumed the form of a duck to kill Krishna?

Q 11 He was Pandu's blind brother who got jealous of his brother's prosperity. Name him?

Q 12 Who taught that the soul could neither be cut, nor be burnt, nor be drenched nor dried?

Answers

1. Krishna
2. He was his mother's cousin brother
3. Kaaliya

4. 7 Children (Krishna was 8th issue)
5. He was Krishna's father
6. She was his mother
7. Yashoda
8. Shakatasur
9. Vrittasur
10. Demon Bakasur
11. Dhritarastra
12. Lord Krishna

Quiz 6

Lord Ganesh

Q 1 What does the word "Ganesh" mean?

Q 2 Who is Lord Ganesh's mother?

Q 3 Who is Lord Ganesh's father?

Q 4 What does the term "Umaputra" mean?

Q 5 Who is the youngest son of Shiva and Parvati?

Q 6 Who is called the elephant head?

Q 7 How many arms does Ganesh have?

Q 8 On which vehicle does Lord Ganpati ride?

Q 9 Lord Ganesh is called 'Vidya Varidhi, Buddhi Vidhata'. What does this phrase mean?

Q 10 On which auspicious occasion do people worship Lord Ganesh's symbol, the elephant.

Answers

1. Head of the group
2. Parvati
3. Shankar

4. Son of Uma (Parvati)
5. Lord Ganesh
6. Lord Ganesh
7. Four
8. Mouse
9. Repertory of Knowledge and God of wisdom
10. Ganesh Chaturthi

Quiz 7

Goddess Lakshmi

Q 1 Which goddess is considered the Demigod of Wealth?

Q 2 Who is Goddess Lakshmi's husband?

Q 3 On which festival is Goddess Lakshmi worshipped by the Hindus?

Q 4 Who planted the celestial tree called "Paarijata" in his garden?

Q 5 Who adorns the moon on his head?

Q 6 On which flower does Goddess Lakshmi sit?

Q 7 Besides Diwali, which festival is celebrated to propitiate the Goddess of Wealth, Lakshmi?

Q 8 Which God is worshipped along with Lakshmi on Diwali?

Q 9 In which part of Delhi is Lakshmi Narayana temple situated?

Q 10 What is the name of temple situated in Ellora Caves?

Answers

1. Lakshmi
2. Narayana

3. Diwali
4. God Indra
5. Lord Shiva
6. Lotus
7. Kojagara
8. Lord Ganesh
9. Connaught Place
10. Lakshmi Narayana temple

Quiz 8

Ganga

Q 1 Who was King Shantanu's first wife?

Q 2 Who was Bheeshma's mother?

Q 3 What was Ganga's first condition, when king Shantanu proposed marriage to her?

Q 4 What was Ganga's second condition for marriage with Shantanu?

Q 5 In which state is Haridwar situated?

Q 6 Lord Vishnu had three wives. Two of them were Ganga and Lakshmi. Name the third wife?

Q 7 The Kalighat temple is situated near the River Ganga. Which Goddess is worshipped in this temple?

Q 8 On the banks of which river, is holy city Varanasi situated?

Q 9 Baijnath Dham is situated on the banks of Holy River Ganga. Name the state in which it is situated?

Q 10 On which personality did the renowned poet Ovid write the following lines: —

"Whose conquests through the orient are renowned,

Where Tawny India is by Ganga bound."

Answers

1. Ganga
2. Ganga
3. That he shall not try to identify her
4. That he shall not try to control her movements
5. U.P. (Uttar Pradesh)
6. Saraswati
7. Kali
8. Ganga
9. Bihar
10. Alexander

Quiz 9

Navagrahas

Q 1 What is the meaning of the term "Navagrahas"?

Q 2 Which planet is the ruler of the Sign Leo?

Q 3 Which planet is the ruler of the Sign Cancer?

Q 4 Which planet is the ruler of two signs—Aries and Scorpio?

Q 5 Which planet is the ruler of two signs—Gemini and Virgo?

Q 6 Which planet is the ruler of two signs—Sagittarius and Pisces?

Q 7 Which planet is the ruler of two signs—Taurus and Libra?

Q 8 Which planet is the ruler of two signs—Capricorn and Aquarius?

Q 9 Which God is believed to have swallowed the sun?

Q 10 Which utensil did Sun-God provide to Draupadi when she was sent along with her husbands to spend 13 years of exile in forests?

Q 11 Which Planet God is the Son of Moon?

Q 12 For which planet God is this Mantra (incantation) chanted—

"Om Hraam Hreem Hraun Shree Suryah Namah"?

Q 13 For which planet God is this Mantra chanted—

"Om Shram Shreem Shraus, Shree Chandraya Namah"?

Q 14 For which planet God is this Mantra chanted—

"Om Kraan Kreen Kraeen, Shree Bhaymaya Namah"?

Q 15 For which planet God is this Mantra chanted—

"Om Braan Breen Braun, Shree Budhaya Namah"?

Answers

1. Nine Planets
2. Sun
3. Moon
4. Mars
5. Mercury
6. Jupiter
7. Venus
8. Saturn
9. Hanuman
10. A Pot
11. Mercury
12. Sun
13. Moon
14. Mars
15. Mercury

Quiz 10

Atharva Veda

Q 1 What does the word "Veda" mean?

Q 2 How many hymns does Atharva Veda contain?

Q 3 How many verses does Atharva Veda contain?

Q 4 Agni is the Chief God of (a) Atmosphere (b) Air (c) Earth.

Q 5 Who is the Chief God of Atmosphere? (a) Soma (b) Indra (c) Saraswati

Q 6 What does the term "Kena Sukta" mean?

Q 7 What does the term Pitris mean?

Q 8 What does the term "Tamas" mean?

Q 9 Shilachi is a (a) Gem (b) Medicinal plant (c) Flower.

Q 10 Soma is a (a) Herb (b) Tree (c) Ocean.

Answers

1. Knowledge
2. 750 hymns
3. 6000 verses
4. Earth
5. Indra
6. From what
7. Ancestors
8. Darkness
9. (b) Medicinal Plant
10. (a) Herb

Quiz 11

Linga Purana

Q 1 A Tirtha is a (a) Herb (b) Tree (c) Place of pilgrimage.

Q 2 Who belongs to the first of four classes? (a) Kshtariyas (b) Sudras (c) Brahmans

Q 3 There are four "Yugas". Three of them are Satya Yuga, Treta Yuga, Dwapar Yuga. Which is the fourth one?

Q 4 Brahma emerged out of a (a) Flower (b) Seed (c) Egg.

Q 5 Yoga means meeting of Soul with (a) Sun (b) Moon (c) Supreme Soul.

Q 6 Jalandhare was a (a) Demon (b) Demigod (c) Human being.

Q 7 How many name's does Lord Shiva have?

(a) 100 (b) 1000 (c) 10,000

Q 8 Who was Parvati's mother?

Q 9 What is the meaning of the term Asura?

Q 10 What do you mean by the term 'Brahman'?

Answers

1. (a) Place of Pilgrimage
2. (c) Brahmans
3. Kaliyug
4. Egg
5. (c) Supreme Soul
6. (a) Demon
7. (b) 1000 names
8. Maneka
9. Demon
10. Divine essence that is regarded as the cause of universe

Quiz 12

Brahmanda Purana

Q 1 How many shlokas does Brahmanda Purana have?

Q 2 Which animal was the mother of Vedavyasa? (a) Fish (b) Duck (c) Mare

Q 3 Creation of the world takes place during Brahma's (a) Day (b) Night

Q 4 Destruction of the world takes place during Brahma's (a) Night (b) Day

Q 5 In how many regions did Brahma divide the world?

Q 6 How many oceans were created by Lord Brahma?

Q 7 What was the name of the tree with miraculous powers that supplied whatever was wished for?

Q 8 The names of the twelve months are Magha, Falguna, Chaitra, Vaishakha, Jyaishtha, Ashada, Shravana, Bhadra, Ashvina, Kartika, Agrahayana and what next?

Q 9 What is formed, when the sun suck up water from the oceans?

Q 10 Destruction comes to those who follow the path of (a) Righteousness (b) Evil

Answers

1. 18 thousand Shlokas
2. (a) Fish
3. (a) Day
4. (a) Night
5. 7 regions
6. 7 oceans
7. Kalpavrikshas
8. Pousha
9. Cloud
10. Evil

Quiz 13

Vamana Purana

Q 1 Lord Shiva is called Simutaketa because he used to live in (1) Mountains (b) Cloud (c) Huts

Q 2 Who was Lord Shiva's father-in-law?

Q 3 Who was Ahalya's father? (a) Shiva (b) Daksha (c) Vishnu

Q 4 From which disease did Shiva suffer from? (a) Cough (b) Asthma (c) Belching

Q 5 Who was Andhak's father?

Q 6 "Vajra" is the name of the terrible weapon owned by (a) Brahma (b) Shiva (c) Indra

Q 7 Who killed Demon Karambha when he was performing meditation under water?

Q 8 She was a beautiful goddess born in Katayani's cottage. What was her name?

Q 9 Which weapon did Lord Shiva give to Goddess Katayani?

Q 10 Which god floated in the form of Dwarf on the River Devika?

Answers

1. (b) Cloud
2. Daksha
3. (b) Daksha
4. (c) Belching
5. Hiranyakshapu
6. (c) Indra
7. Lord Indra
8. Katayani
9. Trident (Trishul)
10. Lord Vishnu

Quiz 14

Markandeya Purana

Q 1 Which is the longest Purana?

Q 2 In which yuga did King Harishchandra live?

Q 3 Who asked King Harishchandra to donate entire kingdom to him?

Q 4 Who was Harishchandra's noble-hearted wife?

Q 5 What was the name of the person who bought King Harishchandra as a slave?

Q 6 What was the name of King Harishchanda's son, who died of snakebite?

Q 7 Who cursed Vishwamitra to become a bird?

Q 8 Who restored Vishwamitra back to his original form, after he was cursed by Sage Vashishtha to become a bird? (a) Brahma (b) Vishnu (c) Shiva

Q 9 For what sin Sumati had to spend 100 years in a hell full of flames?

Q 10 What is the meaning of "Ashvamedha Yagya"?

Answers

1. Skanda Purana
2. Treta Yuga
3. Vishvamitra
4. Shaivya
5. Pravira
6. Rohitashva
7. Vashishtha
8. (a) Brahma
9. For preventing cows to drink water from a well.
10. Horse sacrifice

Quiz 15

The Kurma Purana

Q 1 Which god created a powerful being out of his body to kill Hiranyakshapu?

Q 2 Who became king after the death of Hiranyakshapu?

Q 3 Which form did Lord Vishnu adopt to kill Hiranyakshapu?

Q 4 Who was the eldest son of Vali?

Q 5 How many sons did Vali possess?

Q 6 In which Yuga does sin expand limitlessly?

Q 7 A linga is an image of (a) Vishnu (b) Brahma (c) Shiva.

Q 8 Who possessed the wonderful weapon Sudarshan Chakra?

Q 9 The first stage of life is (a) Brahmacharya (b) Grahasthya (c) Vanaprastha.

Q 10 The third stage of life is (a) Grahasthya (b) Sanyasa (c) Vanaprastha.

Answers

1. Vishnu
2. His brother Hiranyaksha
3. A Boar's
4. Vana
5. Hundred
6. Kaliyug
7. Shiva
8. Vishnu
9. (a) Brahmacharya (studenthood)
10. (c) Sanyasa (barring oneself from everything)

Quiz 16

Vayu Purana

Q 1 Mount Kailash is the dwelling place of (a) Vishnu (b) Brahma (c) Shiva

Q 2 The smallest unit of time is (a) Nimesha (b) Kashtha (c) Kala

Q 3 How many regions of underworld are mentioned in the "Vayu Purna"?

Q 4 Who were known as Adityas?

Q 5 Who were known as Daityas (Demons)?

Q 6 Who hung upside down for one-lakh years to meditate on Brahma?

Q 7 How many sons did the King Vrinadashva have?

Q 8 Atri was a powerful sage. For how many years did he perform Tapasya (Meditation on God)?

Q 9 Who was Chandra's father?

Q 10 How many wives did Yayati have?

Answers

1. (c) Shiva
2. (a) Nimesha
3. Seven
4. Aditi's sons
5. Diti's sons
6. Hiranyakshapu
7. 21,000 sons
8. 3 thousand year
9. Atri
10. Two

Quiz 17

General Quiz on Religion

Q 1 God is limitless treasure of energy that can create, operate and destroy the entire universe within a fraction of a second. His form is similar to (a) Moon (b) Star (c) Sun

Q 2 Shreemad Bhagwat mentions around (a) twenty-one (b) twenty-two (c) twenty-three Avatars of Lord Vishnu.

Q 3 Sanathan Dharma texts mentions around (a) 10 (b) 11 (c) 12 major Avatars of Lord Vishnu.

Q 4 The Man-Lion was the incarnation of (a) Lord Brahma (b) Lord Shiva (c) Lord Vishnu

Q 5 Who killed the mighty Demon Kansa?

Q 6 What name is given to the spiritual being who removes the cause of sorrow? (a) Baushira (b) Rudra (c) Amritah

Q 7 Sattva means (a) Passion (b) Goodness (c) Ignorance

Q 8 Rajas means (a) Passion (b) Goodness (c) Ignorance

Q 9 Tamas means (a) Passion (b) Goodness (c) Ignorance

Q 10 Whose attendant was "Nandi"? (a) Lord Shiva (b) Lord Vishnu (c) Lord Brahma

Q 11 She used to be an insect, who became a princess of Kashi in the next birth, due to her devotion to (a) Lord Shiva (b) Lord Vishnu (c) Lord Brahma

Q 12 "Daityas" is a category of (a) Gods (b) Demons

Q 13 Who was followed by the Army of Monkeys?

(a) Lord Krishna (b) Lord Rama (c) Lord Shiva

Q 14 What does the term "Samudra Manthana" mean?

Q 15 What was the age of Goddess Parvati when her father Himalaya took her to the place when Shiva was meditating? (a) Twenty years (b) Eight years (c) Thirty years

Q 16 He is the God of Love who carries a bow made out of flowers. Name him.

Q 17 What is the name of Fire God?

Q 18 Who was the Son of Agni? (a) Skanda (b) Indra (c) Shaka

Q 19 "Gandharvas" are (a) Singers of Heaven (b) Dancers of Heavens (c) Attendants of Kubera.

Q 20 Which eye does Shiva open up in anger?

Q 21 "Surabhi" is the name of a heavenly (a) Elephant (b) Cow (c) Parrot

Q 22 Who was Vali's father?

Q 23 Who came in the form of a Dwarf, when Vali was the King?

Q 24 How many lingas did Vishvakarma construct for Skanda?

Q 25 Name the Kingdom of Demon Ravana?

Q 26 What was the name of the dreaded serpent that had polluted the River Yamuna, during Kansa's reign?

Q 27 Which musical instrument did Lord Krishna play to attract young girls?

Q 28 What would Krishna steal to tease his lovers?

Q 29 Subhadra was Arjun's wife. She was also the sister of (a) Shiva (b) Indra (c) Krishna.

Q 30 In which state is Partha Sarathy Temple situated?

Q 31 Lord Krishna descends for the protection of (a) evil doers (b) righteous ones

Q 32 What is a Brahma's day called?

Q 33 What term has been given to the technique of control of breath?

Q 34 A practitioner of meditation acquires many powers. One of them is the power to acquire whatever object he desires from anywhere in the three worlds. What is it named?

Q 35 The power to travel anywhere in the world is called (a) Laghima (b) Mahima (c) Ahima.

Q 36 The power to control all the elements in the universe is called (a) Prapti (b) Mahima (c) Ahima.

Q 37 What is indicated when the dogs cry continuously before some body's house? (a) Birth of someone (b) Death of someone

Q 38 Many God's live on mountain peaks. Indra's residence lies on the peak called.........

Q 39 Who is the King of Birds, according to Brahmanda Purana?

Q 40 Who was the father of Sughriva?

Q 41 Which underworld is covered with Sugar?
(a) Gabhastala (b) Mahatala (c) Shritala

Q 42 In which underworld does great Snake Vasuki lives?
(a) Gabhastala (b) Mahatala (c) Shritala

Q 43 Which underworld is blood-like in colour? (a) Atala (b) Sutala (c) Nitala

Q 44 Mercury has a chariot that is drawn by (a) eight-white horses (b) 9 white horses (c) 10 white horses.

Q 45 God of death is called (a) Kali (b) Kala (c) Kalika.

Q 46 Name the mountain in which Shiva and Parvati got married.

Q 47 One of the names denoted to Lord Ganesh is "Gajaanana". What does the term "Gajaanana" mean?

Q 48 The "Mahavir Jayanti" is celebrated as the birthday of (a) Ram (b) Ganesh (c) Hanuman.

Q 49 What was Hanuman's original name?

Q 50 Who jumped the sea in one leap to reach Lanka?

Q 51 Which gift did Hanuman receive as a token of their help to Lord Ram in the battle of Lanka?

Q 52 Dwarakadheesha Temple is situated in ....

Q 53 For whom is this invocation chanted: –

"Seesa-Mukuta Kati Kachhari Ura Vaijaynti Mal,

Yana Banak mo man Baso Sada Biharilal."

Q 54 What does the term "Siddha" mean?

Q 55 What does the term "Amritah" mean?

Q 56 What does the term "Vasudeva" mean?

Q 57 The withdrawal of mind from sense objects is called (a) Dharna (b) Dhyan (c) Pratyahara.

Q 58 Who was the mother of Apsaras? (a) Muni (b) Arishta

Q 59 Who is called Bhooteshwar?

Q 60 Which God roams around in the company of ghosts? (a) Vishnu (b) Brahma (c) Shiva

Q 61 Which is the beloved ornament of Lord Shiva?

Answers

1. (c) Sun
2. (a) Twenty one
3. (a) Ten
4. (c) Lord Vishnu
5. Lord Krishna
6. (b) Rudra
7. (b) Goodness
8. (a) Passion
9. (c) Ignorance

10. (a) Lord Shiva
11. (a) Lord Shiva
12. (b) Demons
13. (b) Lord Rama
14. To churn the ocean
15. (b) Eight years
16. Madana
17. Agni
18. (a) Skanda
19. (a) Singer of the heavens
20. Third eye
21. (c) Cow
22. Demon Virochana
23. Lord Vishnu
24. 3 lingas
25. Lanka
26. Kaliya
27. Flute
28. Butter
29. (c) Krishna
30. Tamil Naidu
31. (b) righteous ones
32. Kalpa
33. Pranayam
34. Anima
35. (a) Laghima
36. (a) Prapti

37. (b) Death of someone
38. Shitanta
39. Garuda
40. Garuda
41. Mahatala
42. Shritala
43. (c) Nitala
44. (a) Eight white horses
45. (b) Kala
46. Mount Kailash
47. Elephant faced
48. (c) Hanuman
49. Maruti
50. Hanuman
51. Pearl necklace
52. Dwarka
53. Lord Krishna
54. Ever-Evident
55. Immortal
56. The abode of all beings
57. (c) Pratyahara
58. (a) Muni
59. Lord Shiva
60. Shiva
61. Rudraksha

Indian Culture and Traditions

India is a land of varied cultures and traditions. Some of them are extremely beneficial for the upliftment of the soul and the physical well being of the mankind. Come; Let's gain knowledge of beneficial cultures and traditions, in order to lead a healthy, wealthy and happy life in this world and the world beyond, after death.

Relevance of Morning Hours

According to Hindu Scriptures, the morning hours between 4 O'clock to 5:30 A.M. are very auspicious. The air consists of 41% oxygen, 55% Nitrogen and 4% carbon-di-oxide. This unpolluted air is extremely beneficial for the mental and physical health. If one takes 100 deep breaths in the morning air, his life span increases and he lives a reasonably long and healthy life in the world. The 4'O'clock time is especially auspicious. At this time, spiritual vibrations envelop the environment and all prayers with good intention are fulfilled if one prays continuously for a few days. One of our servants told the relevance of 4 a.m. She told us that, her children were suffering from small pox and no medicines were available to treat that disease. Finally, she left everything on God and began to pray at 4 a.m. every day. After a few days, her children got rid of small pox completely with the blessings of God. 4 a.m. is a wonderful time. The dreams that occur at sharp 4 a.m. usually become true. One day my mother saw a dream at 4 a.m. She saw the death of my maternal grand mother. After a few days, my maternal grandmother died.

Another dream that my mother narrates is that, she was undergoing some difficult problem and she got the solution of that problem on the next morning itself through a dream.

Relevance of 108 beads in the nacklace

108 is an auspicious number as per the Hindu scriptures. A person takes 21600 breaths in a day out of which 12 hours are spent on materialist activities. Only 12 hours are left to chant the holy name of Almighty God, which means only 10800 breaths could be utilized to take God's name but its difficult to devote so much of time in God's name and thus, keep the number 108 for the chanting of our creator's name.

Non-Veg Food is Harmful for Health

All the religious scriptures mention that, it is a sin to kill innocent animals, which are useful for the mankind. The Hen is a useful animal. It gives eggs. Thus, it should not be killed by the people. The hen does not harm anyone. The harmful animals like Tiger and Leapord may be eliminated, as they cause havoc in the lives of people if their population increases beyond limits. As a person who kills others are hanged to death, the same way the killer of animals should be killed. But the innocent animals like hens and ducks should not be killed. They are innocent. They don't harm people. But though they are innocent, yet they must be controlled. If their population increases beyond limits and the human beings feel uncomfortable in that highly populated environment, then strict steps must be taken to control the rise in their population.

Non-veg food is harmful for health. It can be the cause of many diseases including mental ailments. It makes the person cruel and violent. The emotion of compassion towards other beings eliminates after taking non-veg food. A person can substitute delicious foods like Shahi Paneer, Koftas, Pizzas etc. instead of Meat. There are delicious foods life fruit chaat, fruit creams etc. available in the market, which are good substitute for Meat.

You can make fruit chaat at home by chopping two fruits of your choice, adding a pinch of pepper, a pinch of salt, a spoon of sugar and a lemon. Mingle them together for two-three minutes and have a treat with your beloved ones.

Eat fresh fruits and raw vegetables to keep yourself healthy and fit.

How to Chant Incantation

The Incantations (Mantras) are very beneficial to attain success, wealth, health and happiness in the world. Every mantra has its own benefits. Since the demigods are bestowed with different powers by Almighty God, therefore every demigod blesses the human beings in different ways. Goddess Saraswati bestows knowledge, God Ganpati removes hurdlers to success, Goddess Lakshmi showers wealth, Brahma, Shiva and Vishnu have more powers than other demigods, therefore they can grant all kinds of boons, except salvation to the human-being. Salvation is possible only with the name of Almighty God, or utterance of holy hymn "OM". Lord Brahma, Lord Vishnu and Lord Shiva are also created and destroyed again and again by Almighty Lord, who is in the form of soothing blissful light and is a reservoir of energy.

To chant incantation, one must sit in a lonely noiseless place. Thereafter chant the incantations with utmost devotion and regard to the demigod. Before chanting the incantation, pray to god, what do you want as a blessing from him. It is essential to chant at least one-lakh incantations for good results. After that, for more effective results do Havan (spiritual chanting done before the fire). After that, utter prayers what do you want from God. Thereafter distribute Prasad (holy good) to the poor people.

How to Chant "OM"

"OM" is a wonderful incantation. It is the most simple way to come in proximity with God. The chant of "OM" reduces the burden of sins in our lives. And the negativity of sins that causes sufferings and punishments, obviously reduces with its chant. In fact, it's a known truth that sins are the cause of sufferings. The sins could only be washed away through spiritual processes like meditation, chanting of God's names and so on. The chanting of OM is one of the most simple ways to uplift the soul and reduce the burden of sins.

"OM" should be chanted in the early morning for better results. To get more effective results, one should close one's eyebrows and see in the midst of eyebrows while chanting OM.

Significance of Fast

The Hindus keep fasts to obtain boons from demigods. The demigods get pleased through fasts and they grant boons to their devotees, according to their desires and demands. Besides this, fasts are also kept for physical well-being. Most of the people take juices and fruits on the day of their fast. The old people of weak constitution must not keep fast. It may harm their health. Fast is otherwise very beneficial for health. It gives rests to all organs and the organs function more efficiently as the result of it. The fast also enhances the ability to have control over one's senses.

Significance of Important Symbols

Some symbols like 卐 (Swastik) and ॐ (OM) are very auspicious for our well-being. These kinds of positive symbols should be drawn on the doors of every room of the house. Try to draw as many you can, as these symbols eliminate the negative affects of the house and bring happiness in your lives.

Hindu Marriage Rituals

It is rightly said that marriages are made in heaven. In fact, we don't meet our would-be life-partners, by chance, but they are destined to be our life partner. We only get married to the person, who is written in our lifelines. Our destiny is made according to our performance in the past lives. Sometimes, God changes our destinies for our good, if we utter regular prayers to him. The Hindus celebrate the marriage with great pomp and show in luxurious gardens, houses, or temples. Poor people celebrate them on the roads. A few people match the horoscopes of their children to get them married, but this way they lose good opportunities. No astrologer in the world can predict the future of anybody. They can only tell ten to twenty percent correct things, according to the planetary conditions affecting the lives of the people but they are not accurate, therefore one can't get accurate results through horoscopes. The best way is to match the temperaments and qualifications instead of matching horoscopes. Only God is the best Astrologer, who can predict your future and your future can change with good deeds and sincere prayers. Secondly, it is called an ill-omen, if someone dies on the marriage occasion. Some people break marriages considering it an ill-omen, but it is wrong of them to do so. You may lose good grooms and brides by breaking marriages on such kinds of superstitions The best way to make a marriage successful is to keep on doing havans and prayers after every 6 months. That would bring prosperity and happiness in the lives of husbands and wives and keep them away from irrelevant superstitions and ill-omens.

How to perform last rites?

Whatever might be our customs and traditions, we must take care of the following points while performing the last rites of the person.

(1) After the performance of other rituals, we should add the incantation of Gayatri Mantra for one lakh times, in the name of the deceased, so that he could gain freedom from the miseries of hell. We must utter sincere prayers for the deceased after the completion of 1 lakh of Gayatri incantation.

(2) We must give some charities/donations to the really needy people. We must tell others too to pray for the deceased for sometime, after his death.

With these methods, the deceased person gets relief from the miseries of hell and his soul dwells in peace or gets a new birth, as the command of the God.

Why should we Forgive Others

Forgiveness is a great blessing. God doesn't love a person who keeps on taking revenge from other, but he loves those who correct others and forgive. Lord Buddha forgave the dacoit "Angulimaal" who wanted to kill him, Lord Jesus forgave all the evil-doers who hanged him, Guru Gobind Singh forgave all the cruel people who killed his innocent sons, Sai Baba forgave people who abused and mocked at him, all the spiritual entities, who achieved lofty heights in spiritualism practiced forgiveness. Forgiveness is a virtuous deed. God forgives the sins of those people who forgive others. Some people are very shrewd. They don't acknowledge the virtuous deeds of their beneficent, instead of being thankful to them, they insult, mock and tease them, the tortured person becomes revengeful and he begins to tease and laugh at their behaviour. But the term "Revenge" is offensive. One should not be revengeful. One may use different ways to correct different types of people, but once the person is corrected, he should be forgiven, without second thoughts. One may use different strategies to correct others, but with a spirit of forgiveness not revenge. Remember that God shall only forgive you if you forgive others, else nobody in the world would forgive your wrongs, not even Almighty God.

What is Right and What is Wrong

Many of us are losing the discretion ability to judge what is right and what is wrong, this is the sole reason why chaos has occurred in the society, leaving people bereft of right thought and action.

The people of the world are becoming confused day by day, as they consider right as wrong and wrong as right.

Women are the most tortured and exploited of all. She is suppressed, exploited, misguided, condemned, raped, mocked and teased by the mean men of the society. At home, the men treat them like servants, outside, they misguide them and make them prostitutes, thereafter they defame them. Other than this, the old ladies also start defaming young girls, instead of correcting them and making them tread on the righteous path. The people who have somewhat more sense than other people, don't teach them sense but instead of that, mock and defame them in the society. This is a great sin, that they are committing on woman. They commit great blunders themselves but don't forgive the small mistakes of even most characterful and virtuous women. God's wrath befalls over such men and women who torture young girls and put wrong blames on them. They get severe punishments for such actions. Young girls should be dealt with love and respect, they should not be treated like dirt. The man is not adopting the moderate approach towards women. He is also not able to discriminate between right and wrong. Here are some ways to discriminate between right and wrong.

(1) Ignore the trifles of others, after correcting them. For instance, if your daughter-in-law does not wake up in the morning as she slept late at night due to overwork, give her enough time to sleep. If your daughter-in-law invites her friends at home, let her do so. Teach her not to do things beyond a limit. Going to an outing once a week is fine, but she should not go for a picnic everyday. Things should not be done in an extreme way. Don't eat too much, don't sleep beyond eight hours, don't be too much familiar to anyone and don't go for a picnic everyday. Teach these lessons to yourself and your daughter-in-law lovingly.

(2) Don't find faults in your daughter-in-law always. Ignore her trifles and let her do her work comfortably.

(3) Don't pamper your children too much. They shall get spoilt. Make them discriminate between right and wrong and scold them if they behave arrogantly and don't obey elders' good advices.

(4) Keep yourself at others platform. Scrutinize what shall be your reaction, if someone troubles you, and put wrong blames on you, won't you be hurt. The same way, if you keep condemning innocent people for trifles, and put wrong blames on others, put him/her down, he too shall be hurt. To hurt

innocent people is a great sin. Therefore you may correct shrewd people, but don't hurt innocent. You shall have to suffer severe punishments for the same.

Pyramids—The way to success

Pyramid can bring abundant success in our lives, if used in a right way. The pyramid is a particular kind of shape made up by four equal triangles. This shape is full of divine energy. It can bring abundant success if used in a right way. Many experiments by great scientists have portrayed that pyramids do contain divine energy, which may be called electro magnetic energy, made up of electric and magnetic particles that could fulfil every wish placed under it and eliminate all kinds of diseases.

To conduct a test, you may keep a set of ten pyramids near a seriously sick person. He/she will recover soon, if you shall also give her pyramid water to drink. To charge water, you may keep a glass of water for 12 hours under a pyramid. After 12 hours, it shall get charged by the divine energy of pyramid. Give it daily to the diseased patients. You will get to observe the wonders of pyramid yourself. If you keep a pyramid on the stomach of a person suffering from gastroenteritis, his/her gas tends to reduce, gradually. In spite of all this, we must know the truth, that pyramids don't give thick results. But if applied in a right way, they may give best results. If you go to see the pyramids of Egypt, you shall find that the dead bodies of people who died thousands of years back have not decayed with time. So, which energy preserves their bodies, and keeps them without decay for years together? It's of course the divine energy of the pyramid. If you want your wishes to be fulfilled, then you may write your wish in a piece of paper and keep it under a pyramid. Your wish shall be fulfilled, if it doesn't harm or hurt anyone in the world.

Therefore, you may derive the benefits of the divine energy available in abundance in the shape of pyramid. Keep a set of ten pyramids with the word "OM" inscribed on them, in each room of your house. This way all the negativity of your house shall eliminate gradually and your sufferings, troubles and tribulations shall also reduce with the blessings of Almighty God.

Attribute beauty in Thought and Action

We people are becoming rough and tough these days. We don't show courtesy to others. I remember just sometime back I was travelling in a bus, when I saw a young man misbehaving with an old person. He was rudely telling the old person to get aside, whereas the old person said that he was already at a corner, and there was no space left to get aside; moreover, he was suffering from an ailment. The young main rudely retorted back that what should he do if he was suffering from an ailment. I was shocked by his words. I chided the man and requested someone to get a seat for the old man. Thereafter a man gave a seat to the old man and the old man looked with gratitude at me, as if I was his own daughter, who helped him. I also scolded the young man adding that if you shall not help others, then who shall help you when you are in need? I have seen many people fighting in the bus on trifles.

One day, an old man told a lady to give the seat to him as he was a senior citizen and that seat was reserved for senior citizens. The woman started fighting with the man. I told the woman to some to my seat instead of fighting with the man. The woman however did not allow me to stand and stopped fighting after that.

One other day, a man saw a woman occupying two seats in a bus. He told her rudely to give them one of the seats. The woman didn't say anything but a man who might be her brother or husband began to quarrel with the man for speaking rudely to that woman, as she was sick. A fight occurred between them. I told the rude man to be quiet as she was a woman and that too sick. The man somehow, became quiet and stopped fighting with the sick woman.

What I intend to say is that people have become proud and selfish, that is why we are not respected and loved by others. Don't we have enough courtesy to behave in a manner, that innocent people don't get hurt by our behaviour.

We may speak out whatever is there in our mind, but lovingly and politely. Whenever I want to request someone to give my mother a ladies seat, I request him politely saying "Brother, these seats are reserved for ladies. She is an old woman. Kindly give her a seat". My request is usually granted by the men, as my tone is polite and attitude is loving.

If we want love and respect from others, then we must add the virtues of politeness, kindness, selflessness and courtesy in our lives, only then can we expect love and regards from others, otherwise not.

Avoid Misunderstandings

Most of the relations break due to misunderstandings. Misunderstandings bring unnecessary quarrels and conflicts in the families, between friends, relations and acquaintances. They create enemies for no rhyme or reason. Just imagine if a benevolent person helps a sick man out of compassion and the sick man thinks he is doing so out of greed. He is helping him to acquire his property. Now the sick man defames the benevolent man in the society. The kind-hearted person is annoyed by the sick man for defaming him in spite of his good behaviour. He breaks relations with the sick man and the sick man keeps on repenting for having lost a good friend, who always helped him in due need.

Due to misunderstandings, people lose a good friend. These kind of people keep on appreciating shrewd people who cheat them and condemn good-hearted people. By misunderstanding the feelings of a good man, you tend to lose a great helper, therefore try to understand the feelings of others in a right way. The misunderstandings cause quarrels and conflicts and lead a person to degradation, attributing miseries in his life.

Do Good without Obligation

These days people oblige others for small things. If one gives a five rupee note to a poor man, he would oblige him for a hundred of times for as small amount as a five rupee note, if a host serves food to a guest, he would oblige him for a thousand times, if a friend gives a small gift to another friend, she would keep on telling to all that she has given a gift to her. This is the wrong attitude of people. They oblige others for small things. In fact, it is the duty of a wealthy man to render a little helping hand to a poor man, who is in need. He has been bestowed with the blessing of wealth by God to help others without obligation.

Let's not imitate narrow-minded people who oblige others for small things, instead imitate people like Mother Teresa who helped numerous people in distress without any obligations. It iss wrong to oblige others for small helps, and even more wrong if you seek return of money and gifts that you have given to your beloved ones. It doesn't win your friends but even your friends turn into your enemies. If you want to win over friends then "Do good without obligation".

Glimpses of Gita

Gita is one of the greatest religious scriptures of the world. Lord Krishna has spoken it itself to his disciple Arjuna, to make him practice the principles of life, that purify the soul of the person, uplift the soul and give relief to all sufferings and tribulations. Gita has been spoken not only for Arjuna, but for the benefit of the entire mankind. Here are some selective texts of Gita to enlighten up our souls.

Krishna says—

"As the embodied soul continually passes in this body, from boyhood to youth, and then to old-age, the soul similarly passes to another body at death. The self-realised soul is not bewildered by such a change.

The temporary appearance of heat and coolness, happiness and distress, and their disappearance in due course, are like the appearance and disappearance of winter and summer season. The person who is not disturbed by happiness and distress and is steady in both is certainly eligible for liberation.

That which pervades the entire body is indestructible. No one is able to destroy the imperishable soul.

Only the material body of the indestructible, immeasurable and eternal living entity is subject to destruction.

He who thinks that the living entity is the slayer, or that the entity is slain, does not understand. The scenes are so strong and impetuous, that they forcibly carry away the mind even of a man of discrimination who is endeavouring to control them.

One who restrains his senses and fixes his consciousness upon me is known as a man of steady intelligence.

While contemplating the objects of the senses, a person develops attachment for them and from such attachment lust develops and from lust, anger arises.

From anger, delusion arises and from delusion bewilderment of memory. When memory is bewildered intelligence is lost and when intelligence is lost, one falls down again into the material pool.

One who can control his senses by regulated principles and who is free from attachment and aversion, can obtain the mercy of God.

One who is not in transcendental consciousness can have neither a controlled mind nor steady intelligence, without which there is no possibility of peace and how can there be happiness without peace. A person who has given up all desires for sense gratification who lives free from desires and devoid of false ego–he alone can attain real peace.

Not by merely abstaining from work can one achieve freedom from reaction, nor by renunciation alone can one attain perfection.

One who controls the senses by the mind and engages his active organs in works of devotion, without attachment is by for superior.

In the beginning of the creation, lord of all creatures sent forth generations of men and god, along with sacrifices for

Vishnu, and blessed them by saying "Be thou happy by this sacrifice (yajna), because its performance would bestow upon you all desirable things. The demigods being pleased with sacrifices will also please you, thus, nourishing one-another, there will reign general prosperity for all.

Whatever action a great man performs, common men follow. And whatever standards he sets by exemplary acts, all the world pursues.

As the ignorant perform their duties with attachment to results, so the learned may also act, but without attachment, for the sake of leading, people on the right path. The wise should encourage ignorant people not to refrain from work but to engage in work in the spirit of devotion.

He, who disregards these teachings and doesn't practice them regularly, is to be considered bereft of all knowledge, befooled and doomed to ignorance and bondage. It is lust only which is born out of contact with the material modes of passion, and later transformed into wrath, and which is the all-devouring, sinful enemy of this world.

As fire is covered by smoke, as a mirror is covered by, as the embryo is covered by womb, similarly, the living entity is covered by different degrees of lust.

Therefore, O Arjuna, curb the great symbol of sin (lust) by regulating the senses and slay this destroyer of knowledge and self-realisation. The working senses are superior to dull matter, mind is higher than the senses, intelligence is still higher than the mind and he (the soul) is even higher than intelligence. Thus, knowing oneself to be transcendental to material senses, mind and intelligence, one should control the lower self by the higher self, and, thus—by spiritual strength—conquer this insatiable enemy known as lust.

Whenever and wherever there is a decline in religious practice and a predominant rise of irrigation–at that time, I descend myself.

To deliver the pious and to annihilate the miscreants, as well as to re-establish the principles of religion, I advent myself millennium after millennium.

One who knows the transcendental nature of my appearance and activities does not, upon leaving the body take his birth again in this material world, but attains my eternal abode, O Arjuna.

Being feed from attachment, fear and anger, being fully absorbed in me and taking refuge in me, many, many persons in the past became purified and thus they attained transcendental love for me. All of them as they surrender unto me —I reward accordingly. Everyone follows my path in all respects.

All the liberated souls in ancient times acted with this understanding and so attained liberation. Therefore, as did the ancients, you should perform your duty in this divine consciousness.

A man of understanding acts with mind and intelligence perfectly controlled, gives up all sense of proprietorship over his possessions and acts only for the bare necessities of life.

The work of a man who is unattached to the modes of material nature and who is fully situated in transcendental knowledge merges entirely into transcendence.

A person who is fully absorbed in Krishna, consciousness is sure to attain the spiritual kingdom through his full contribution to spiritual activities for the consummation is absolute and the things offered are also of the same spiritual nature.

Just try to learn the truth by approaching a spiritual master. Infuse from him submissively and render service unto him. The self-realised soul can impart knowledge unto you because he has seen the truth. And when you have learned the truth, you will know living beings are but part of me and that they are in me and are mine.

Even if you are considered to be the most sinful of all sinners, when you are situated in the boat of the transcendental knowledge, you will be able to cross over the ocean of miseries.

As the blazing fire turns wood to ashes, O Arjuna, so does the fire of knowledge burn to ashes all reactions to material activities.

A faithful man who is absorbed in transcendental knowledge and who subdues his senses quickly attains the supreme spiritual peace.

But the ignorant and faithless persons who doubt the revealed scriptures do not attain God consciousness. For the doubting soul there is neither happiness in this world, nor in the next.

The renunciation of work and work in devotion are both good for liberation. But of the two, work in devotional service is better than renunciation of works. One who neither hates nor desires the fruits of activities is known to be always renounced. Such a person, liberated from all dualities, easily overcomes material bondage and is completely liberated, O mighty-armed Arjuna. Unless one is engaged in the devotional service of the lord, mere renunciation of activities cannot make one happy. The sage, purified by works of devotion, achieves the supreme without delay.

One who works in devotion, who is a pure soul and who controls his mind and senses is dear to everyone and everyone is dear to him. Though always working, such a man is never entangled.

A person in the divine consciousness although engaged in seeing, hearing, touching, smelling, eating, moving about, sleeping and breathing, always knows within himself, that he actually does nothing at all. Because while evacuating, receiving, opening, or closing his eyes, he always knows that only the material senses are engaged with their objects and that he is aloof from them. One who performs his duty without attachment, surrendering the results unto the Supreme God is not affected by sinful action, as the lotus leaf is untouched by water.

The steadily devoted soul attains unadulterated peace because he offers the results of all activities to me, whereas a person who is not in harmony with divine, who is greedy for the fruits of his labour, becomes entangled.

When one is enlightened with the knowledge by which nuisance is destroyed, then his knowledge reveals everything as the Sun lights up everything in the day-time.

The humble sage sees with equal vision a learned and gentle brahman, a cow, an elephant, a dog and a dog-eater. One whose happiness in within, who is active within, who rejoices within, and is illumined within, is actually the perfectly mystic. He is liberated in supreme and ultimately he attains supreme.

Those who are free from Anger and all material desires, who are self-realised, self disciplined and constantly endeavouring for perfection are assured liberation in the supreme in the very near future.

Shutting out all external sense objects, keeping the eyes and vision concentrated between the two eyebrows, suspending the inward and outward breaths within the nostrils and thus controlling the mind, senses and intelligence, transcendentalist becomes free from desire, fear and anger. One who is always in this state is certainly liberated.

A man must elevate himself by his own mind not degrade himself. The mind is the friend of the conditioned soul and his enemy as well.

For he who has conquered his mind, it is the best of friends, but for one who has failed to do so, his very mind will be the greatest enemy.

For one who has conquered the mind, the supersoul is already reached, for he has attained tranquillity. To such a man happiness and distress, heat and cold honour and dishonour are all the same.

A person is said to be further advanced when he regards all the well-wishers, friends and enemies, the envious, the pious, the sinner and those who are indifferent and impartial with an equal mind. One should hold one's body neck and head erect in a straight line and stare steadily at the tip of the nose. Thus, with an un-agitated subdued mind, devoid of fear, completely free from sex life, one should meditate upon me within the heart and make me the ultimate goal of life.

By meditating in this manner, always controlling the body, mind and activities, the mystic transcendentalist attains to the kingdom of God.

Those who worship the demigods will take birth among the demigods, those who worship ghosts and spirits will take with among such beings, and those who worship me will live with me.

If one offers me with love and devotion a leaf, a flower, fruit and water, I will accept it.

All that you do, all that you eat, all that you offer and give away as well as all austerities that you may perform, should be done as an offering to me.

Thus, you shall be free of all reactions to good and evil deeds and by this principle of renunciation, you will be liberated and come to me. I envy no one, nor am I partial to anyone, I am equal to all. But whoever renders service unto me in devotion is a friend, is in me, and I am a friend to him. Intelligence, knowledge, freedom from doubt and delusion, forgiveness, truthfulness, self-control, calmness, pleasure and pain, birth, death, fear, fearlessness, non-violence, equanimity, satisfaction, austerity, charity, fame and infancy are created by me, alone.

I am the source of everything, from me the entire creation flows, knowing this, the wise worship me with all their hearts. I am the self, O conquerer of sleep, seated in the hearts of all creatures. I am the beginning, the middle and the end of all beings. Of the Adityas, I am Vishnu, of Lights I am radiant Sun, among Stars I am the Moon.

Of the Vedas, I am Sama Veda, of the demigods I am Indra, of the senses I am the mind, and in living beings I am consciousness. Of vibrations I am the transcendental OM, of sacrifices I am the chanting of the holy names (Japa) and of immovable things, I am Himalayas. But for what need is there, Arjuna for all this detailed knowledge. With a single fragment of myself, I pervade and support this entire universe. Know that all beautiful, glorious and mighty creations, spring but from a spark of my splendour. One who is not envious but is a kindly friend to all creatures who does not think himself a proprietor, who is free from false ego and equal both in happiness and distress, who is always satisfied and engaged in devotional service with determination, and whose mind and intelligence are fixed upon me, he is very dear to me.

He, for whom no one is put into difficulty and who is not disturbed by anxiety, who is steady in happiness and distress is very dear to me.

This body is called a field, and one who knows this body is called the Knower of the field.

I am also the knower of all bodies, and to understand this body and its owner is called knowledge. Humility, Pridelessness, Non-violence, Tolerance, Simplicity, approaching a bonafide spiritual master, cleanliness, stead fastness and self-control, renunciation of the objects of sense-gratification, absence of false ego, perception of evil of birth, death, disease and old age, no-attachment to children, wife, name and so on, and equilibrium of the mind, devotion to the service of the lord, detachment from general mark of people, accepting the importance of self-realisation and philosophical search for the absolute truth, all there are in aggregate called knowledge, and besides this whatever may be is ignorance.

Material nature consists of the three modes–goodness, passion and ignorance. When a living being comes in contact with nature, he becomes conditioned by these modes.

O sinless one, the mode of goodness, being purer than the others is illuminating and frees one from sinful reactions. Those situated in that mode develop knowledge and become conditioned by the sense of happiness. The mode of passion is born of unlimited desires and longings. O son of Kunti and because of this, one is bound to material fruitive activities.

The delusion of all living entities is the mode of ignorance. The results of this mode are madness, indolence and sleep that bind the conditioned soul.

The mode of goodness conditions one to happiness, passion conditions him to the fruits of action and ignorance to madness.

Sometimes the mode of passion becomes prominent, defeating the mode of goodness, sometimes the mode of goodness defeats passion, sometimes the mode of ignorance defeats goodness and passion. In this way, there is ever a competition for supremacy. The manifestation of the mode of goodness can be experienced when all the gates of one's body are illuminated by knowledge.

When there is an increase in the mode of passion, the symptoms of great attachment, uncontrollable desire, hankering and intense endeavour develop.

Where there is an increase in the mode of ignorance, madness, illusion, inertia and darkness are manifested.

When one dies in the mode of goodness, he attains to the pure higher planets.

One who dies in the mode of passion takes birth among those engaged in fruitive activities and one who dies in the mode of ignorance takes birth in the animal kingdom.

By acting in the mode of goodness, one becomes purified. Work done in the mode of passion results in distress and actions performed in the mode of ignorance result in foolishness.

From the modeof goodness, real knowledge develops, from the mode of passion, greed develops and from the mode of ignorance, foolishness, madness and illusion develop.

Those situated in the mode of goodness gradually go upward to the higher planets, those in the mode of passion live on the earthly planets and those in ignorance go down in hellish worlds.

When the embodied being is able to transcend these three dualities he can become free from birth, death, old age and their distress and can enjoy nectar even in this life.

He was neither hates nor desires the development of the three qualities of illumination, attachment and delusion, who is transcendentally situated, remaining neutral through all the reactions of the modes, thinking that they may work but that he is transcendental; he who looks equally upon happiness and distress, upon a pebble, a stone or a piece of gold, who is equal towards the desirable and the undesirable, who is well-situated and steady in defamation and adoration, he who receives honour and dishonour equally, who treats friend and enemy alike and who is not engaged in material activities—he is said to have transcended the three modes of nature.

One who is engaged in full devotional service, unfailing in all circumstances, at once transcends the modes of material nature and thus comes to the level of Brahman (God).

That abode of mine is not illumined by the Sun or Moon, nor by electricity. One who reaches it never comes back to this material world.

The living entities in this conditional world are my fragmental parts and they are eternal but due to conditioned life they are struggling very hard with the sixth senses, which include the mind.

The living entity in the world carries his different conception of life as the air carries aromas. Thus, he takes one kind of body and again quits it to take another.

The living entity, thus, taking another gross body, obtains a particular type of ear, tongue, nose and sense of touch, centred about the mind. He thus enjoys a particular set of sense objects.

The foolish cannot understand how a living entity can quit his body or what sort of body he enjoys under the spell of nature, but one whose eyes are trained in knowledge can see this.

I am seated in everyone's heart, and from me come remembrance, knowledge and forget fullness. By all Vedas, I am to be known. I am the compiler of Vedanta and I know the Vedas as they are.

There are two classes of beings the fallible and the infallible, in the material world every entity is called fallible and in the spiritual world every entity is called infallible.

In this world there are two kinds of created beings. One is called divine and the other demoniac.

Those with demoniac qualities exhibit pride, arrogance, false prestige, anger harshness and ignorance.

The transcendental assets lead to liberation, whereas the demoniac assets are meant for bondage.

Those who are of demoniac quality do not know what is to be done and what is not to be done. They are unclean. They do not know how to behave, nor is there any truth in them. They say that this world is unreal, that there is no foundation and that there is no God in control. It is produced of sex-desire and has no other cause than lust.

Following such conclusions, the demoniac lost to themselves and without intelligence, engage in unbeneficial horrible works meant to destroy the world.

The demoniac person thinks: So much wealth do I have today, and I will gain more according to my schemes. So much is mine now and it will increase in the future, more and more. He is my enemy and I have killed him, and my other enemy will also be killed. I am the Lord of everything, I am enjoyer, I am perfect, powerful and happy. I am the richest man surrounded by aristocratic relatives. There is none so powerful and happy as I am. I shall perform sacrifices. I shall give some charity and thus I shall rejoice. In this way, such persons are deluded by ignorance. Thus perplexed by various anxieties and bound by a network of illusions, one becomes too strongly attached to sense enjoyment and falls down into hell.

Bewildered by fake ego, strength, pride, lust and anger, the demon becomes envious of the Supreme Personality of Godhead, who is situated in his own body and in others.

Because they are envious and mischievous, the lowest of men, I put them back into the ocean of material existence, into various demoniac species of life.

Gaining repealed birth among the species of demoniac life, such person can never approach me. Gradually they sink down to the most abominable position of existence.

There are three gates leading down to hell—lust, anger and greed. Every same person should give these up, for they lead to the degradation of the soul.

One who acts whimsically, not caring for the regulations of the scriptures, can never attain perfection nor happiness, nor the supreme destination.

Men in the mode of goodness worship the demigods, those in the mode of passion worship the demons, and those in the mode of darkness worship the dead and ghosts.

Foods in the mode of goodness increase the duration of life, purify existence, give strength and increase health, happiness and satisfaction. Such foods are juicy and fatty. They are very conducive to the healthy condition of the body.

Food that is too bitter, too sour, too salty, too pungent, to dry, or too hot causes distress, misery and disease. Such food is very dear to those in the mode of passion.

Foods prepared for more than three hours before being eaten, which are tasteless, juiceless and decomposed, which have a bad smell and that consist of remnants and untouchable things are very dear to those in the mode of ignorance.

The imperfect understanding which cannot distinguish between religion and irreligion and which therefore mistakes action to be done with action not to be done is in the mode of passion.

The understanding which considers irreligion to be religion and religion to be irreligion, under the spell of illusion and darkness, striving always in the wrong direction, is said to be in mode of ignorance.

That understanding by which one can recognise which actions should be done and which actions should not be done, what is fearful and what is not fearful, what is binding and what is liberating, is known to be in the mode of goodness. By worship of Lord, who is the source of all beings and who is all-pervading, a man can become perfect while doing his work.

One can obtain the result of renunciation simply by self-control and by becoming unattached to material things and disregarding material enjoyments.

That is the highest perfectional stage of renunciation.

Being purified by his intelligence and controlling the mind with determination, giving up the objects of sense gratification, being greed from attachment and hatred, who eats a small quantity of food, who controls the body and the speaking power, who is free from false ego, lust, anger and acceptance of material things, such a person is certainly elevated to the position of self-realisation.

Surrender unto God in all respects and by his MERCY YOU CAN HAVE TRANSCENDENTAL PEACE AND ATTAIN ETERNALABODE.

A Talk on Religion

(Mr. Singh, Mrs. Upadhyaya, Mrs. Elizabeth are having a discussion on "Religion")

Mr. Singh: I wonder why we people respect other religions, when all the religions teach us good values of life and forbid us from doing wrong.

Mr. Upadhyaya: Every religion teaches one and the same thing "To avoid doing acts that hurt or harm others, they are in fact the cause of all our sufferings and tribulations.

Mrs. Elizabeth: I don't know why we don't understand the truth that God is one and the same. God may have different names, but in spite of that he is one and the same soothing, peaceful, powerful energy in the form of electro-magnetic light.

Mr. Singh: God is so powerful that it can create and destroy innumerable universes within a fraction of a second

Mr. Upadhyaya: You know only a few days back, I met a person, who kept on saying that his religion was the most superior religion of the world.

Mr. Singh: What a funny person? How can any religion be superior to the other religion, when all of them preach one and the same thing: To develop faith in God, meditate on him and chant his names.

Mr. Upadhyaya: Some people are ignorant of this truth. They think that their God is different than other Gods, and therefore they don't respect other religions of the world.

Mrs. Elizabeth: But God is not different. His names are different. Muslims call him "Allah", Hindus call him "Ram" Christians call him "God" and Sikhs call him "Ek Omkar".

Mr. Singh: People refer him with different names, but God is one and the same.

Mr. Upadhyaya: I have a Muslim friend. He is very good-natured otherwise. He always renders me help whenever I am in need, but he doesn't allow me to watch "Ramayan" on T.V. He gets irrigated when I watch Ramayan.

Mrs. Elizabeth: That means he is not evil, but is ignorant. He doesn't have full knowledge about God. In fact, I too had a good friend, who was Muslim. Initially, she never used to talk to me, as I belonged to different religion, but when I poured water of love in her fire of hatred, the fire of hatred cooled down and now, she is my best friend in the world. I always seek moral, mental, social and financial help from her in need, and she never refuses help.

Mr. Upadhyaya: All the messengers of God such as Lord Buddha, Jesus Christ, Prophet Mohammad, Guru Nanak have taught us to keep right intentions for others and do right deeds.

Mrs. Elizabeth: The problem that we are suffering from, is lack of discrimination between right and wrong. We consider wrong as right and right as wrong.

Mr. Singh: Yeah, just take the example of young boys and girls who are losing their character considering that what they are doing is right.

Mr. Upadhyaya: I remember a neighbour who used to condemn his wise wife on her every wise decision. If she told him to stop drinking liquor, he would call her crazy and beat her up. If his wife told him to save money for future, again he would call her foolish and insult her before others. He lost the discrimination between right and wrong, and considered every wrong action as right and right as wrong.

Mr. Singh: This is what all the religions of the world preach. They teach us to discriminate between right and wrong, so that we could lead a healthy, wealth and happy life.

A talk on Self Realisation

(Miss Kapoor and Mrs. Dutta are having a discussion on "Self Realisation")

Miss Kapoor: We are part and parcel of ocean of love, but we have got separated from that ocean due to our limitless desires to achieve materialistic things.

Mrs. Dutta: We have to realise ourselves to mingle with God and become a part of him.

Miss Kapoor: How can we do that?

Mrs. Dutta: There are many ways for realising God. You can chant his names, meditate on him or read holy scriptures.

Miss Kapoor: Which is the best way of "Spiritual Enlightenment"?

Mrs. Dutta: "Meditation is the best way of self realisation.

Miss Kapoor: How to meditate on God?

Mrs. Dutta: Well, the first condition to elevate your soul is cleanliness. You must keep your mind, body and soul, neat and clean. One should not skip bath any day. If we are sick, then, we may wipe our body with a towel dipped in hot water.

After taking a bath, sit in a room, where there is no noise of radio or television, to disturb your spiritual exercise of soul.

After that take a few deep breaths for ten minutes.

Now you feel relaxed and are ready for self-realisation.

Now close your eyes and fix them in between your eyebrows. Your concentration should lie in between your eyebrows.

Now recite the spiritual hymn "OM". Practice this for one hour daily.

Within a span of two months, you could attain spiritual enlightenment if you are sincerely into it.

Miss Kapoor: What are the benefits of meditation?

Mrs. Dutta: There are numerous benefits of meditation. Firstly, it enhances our physical health and keeps the deadly diseases at bay. Secondly, it increases our memory, concentration and ability to discriminate between right and wrong.

Thirdly, it brings us close to God and thus we attain abundant peace, joy and happiness.

Everyday Prayers

We are giving a few beneficial prayers that would help you to reduce the sufferings and tribulations of life. They would help you to achieve glory, success and health. Practice them every day for good results.

Every day Prayer 1

(God)

O Almighty God,

My dearest father,

My beloved mother and the most loving friend.

With utmost humility, I would request you to kindly grant me and my beloved ones, success, wealth, health,

happiness and salvation.

My dearest father, give me your protection

and shelter till your death.

Every day Prayer 2

(Lord Ram's Aarti)

Shree Ramchandra Kripalu bhaj man,

haran bhav-bhaya darunam,

Navakanj-lochan, Kanjamukh, kaj Kanj,
Pada Kanjarunam,
Kandarp aganita amita chhavi,
Navneela-neerad sundaram,
Pat Peeta manahu tarhita ruchi
Shuchi naumi janaksuta varam.
Bhaju deena bhandu dinesh danav,
Daitya vansha nikandanam
Raghunanda Anandakanda Kaushal
Chanda Dashrathanandanam
Sir mukut kundal tilak charu velasang vibhushnam
Ajanbhuj shar–chap–dhar sangram jit khar dooshanam
Iti vadarti Tulsidas Shankar–Shesh–muni–man–ranjnam
Mam Hriday-Kunj niwas Kuru, Kamadi Khal dal ganjanam

Translation: O mind, worship Lord Ram who is ever gracious to his devotees and whose grace can destroy the most deadly mundane afflictions and fears.

He whose eyes look like a blooming Lotus and face like a Lotus flower. His hands are as beautiful as the Lotus and his feet appear like deep Red Lotus flowers, abloom. His this appearance which goes beyond the extent of vision, also pales into insignificance, the combined charms of innumerable Kaamdev and gives the impression of a dark nimbus, with his yellow raiment appearing like the streak of lightening pure and neat. I bow to such captivating appearance of Janak's daughter Sita's groom.

O mind, ever worship the beacon on his head, he has large earrings in his ears and his well endowed body has ornaments adorning its various limbs, in a sleek manner.

His long arms that reach upto his knees, has the bow and arrow with which he had vanquished Khara and Dushan, the demons. Tulsidas says that this form is very captivating to Shankar, Sheshnag and Sages which gives them supreme delight. The poet prays that may this form, that destroys all evils like passion and lust, even dwell in his heart's Lotus.

Every day Prayer 3

(Krishna)

Baso more nainan men Nandalal,

Mor Mukut-Makarakrita Kundal arun tilak diyen bhal,

Mohini Moorat Sanvari Soorat naina bane bisal,

Adhara-Sudha-ras murali rajat ura Vaijantimal,

Chhudra ghantika Kati-tata sobhita, noopur sabad rasal

Meera prabhu santan sukhadayee,

Bhagal bachhal gopal

Says Meerabai: O son of Nanda: Fill up my vision with your image only. That image–a diadem made of peacock's feathers over your head, the crocodile shaped ear-rings dangling from your ear-lobes, a bright red auspicious mark on your forehead, that very captivating visage of dark complexion with the eyes big and bright, a flute emitting mellifluous notes softly, reposing upon your lips, with a comely waist-band adorned with tiny bells and the sweet notes sounding anklets! O gopal, shedding grace upon your devotees, you are the source of happiness to the noble-persons–let your this image be ever before my eyes.

Every day Prayer 4

(Shiva): The form (of Lord Shiva) for Meditation

Dhyayennityam Mahesham rajatagirinibham

charuchandra katamsam,

Ratnakolpojywalangam Para Shumri garvara bheeti
hastam prasannam padmaseenam samantastutana

mamarganeirvyaghra krittim vasanam,

Vishwadyam vishwabeejam nikhila

bhayaharm pancha vaktram trinetram

Translation: He whose body hue is bright like the reflection upon the snowed mountain, who adorns beautiful moon, as though an ornament, whose body is belight with the bejewelled adornments, who has an axe and a deer in his two hands andthe other two are raised to bless and grant freedom from fear, who is happy and sitting upon the Lotus flower, surrounded by gods hymning him, who is clad in panther's skin, who is the root-seed of the creation of the world, who removes all woes and afflictions, who has five faces and three eyes–one should ever meditate on lord's this form.

Everyday Prayer 5

(Vishnu)

Om Jai Jagdeesh hare,

Swami jai jagdeesh hare

Bhakta janon ke sankaat

Kshan mein door kare

Jo dhyave phal pave dukh

Vinashe manke

Sukh sampati ghar ave

Kastha mite tanka

Om jai Jagdish hare

Mata Pita tum mere Sharan gahun mein kiski

Tum bin aur na dooja aas karu main kiski,

Om Jai Jagdeesh Hare

Tum Pooran Parmatma, tum Antaryami,

Parbrahma parmeshwar tum sabke swami

Om Jai Jagdeesh Hare

Tum Karuna ke Sagar Tum palan karta

Main Moorakh khal kami kaipa karo bharta

Om Jai Jagdeesh hare

Tum ho ek Agochar, sabke pranpati

Kis vidhi miloon dayamaya Tum se mein kumati

Om jai Jagdeesh hare

Deenbandhu dukh harta tum rakshak mere, Karuna hasta badhao dwar parah mein tere

Om Jai Jagdeesh Hare

Vishaya Vikar mitao pap haro deva, Shraddha bhakti badahao santan ki seva

Om Jai Jagdeesh Hare

Tan-Man Dhan jo kuch hai sab hee hai tera

Tera tujhko Arpan, Kya Lage Mera

Om Jai Jagdeesh Hare,

Bhakta Janan ke Sankat Kshan mein door Kare.

Om Jai Jagdish Hare

Translation: Chanting the holy monosyllable "OM", we raise the victory slogans of the lord of the world, Hari, who ends all afflictions of his devotees in a trice. He who worships him gets the reward and his distress is destroyed quickly. All happiness and riches come to his home and his entire physical troubles end. O Lord, you are my parents–who else can provide me shelter for I have no one of my own except you. Victory to the lord of the world. You are Supreme God, Lord of all and knower of the secret of every heart. You are an ocean of kindness and sustainer of the world while I am steeped in vices. Please be gracious to me, my master! You are imperishable by senses, yet with you is instinct every life.

How should I approach you, as I am ignorant? O friend of the humble, the redeemer of sorrow, you are my protector. Please extend your merciful hand to raise me as I am lying at your door.

Destroy vice and malice, and eliminate sin from our life. Enhance sense of devotion and loyalty to the noble.

Whatever I have is all yours, which I offer you Lord! Master of the World!